The Barefoot Book of

HEROIC
CHILDREN

For my own heroic children, Elisabeth and Stephan — B. H.
For Grandma Cann with much love — H. C.

Barefoot Books
PO Box 95
Kingswood
Bristol
BS30 5BH

First published in Great Britain in 2000 by Barefoot Books Ltd

This book has been printed on 100% acid-free paper
Illustrations were prepared in watercolour and pen and ink on
Windsor and Newton 260lb cold-pressed paper

Graphic design by Jennie Hoare, Bradford on Avon
Typeset in Giovanni Book 12pt
Colour reproduction by Bright Arts, Singapore
Printed in Hong Kong/China by South China Printing Co. (1988) Ltd.

ISBN 1 902283 22 8

British Cataloguing-in-Publication Data:
a catalogue for this book is available from the British Library

1 3 5 7 9 8 6 4 2

ACKNOWLEDGEMENTS
Thank you to Braulio Gonzales for suggesting the theme of this book,
and regrets for not being able to include *los ni-os* heroes of Mexico. Thank you to
Catherine Hopkins and the grades five and six of Shannon Park Elementary School
for suggesting Sadako Sasaki. Thanks to my publisher, Tessa Strickland,
and my copy-editor, Kate Parker, to Jennie Hoare, who designed this book, and
to the many librarians in both the public and university libraries I haunted.
And many thanks to my tireless family, especially Mark.

The Barefoot Book of
HEROIC
CHILDREN

written by
REBECCA HAZELL

illustrated by
HELEN CANN

walk
the way of wonder...
Barefoot Books

CONTENTS

INTRODUCTION

Do you ever feel that the whole world is run by people who are bigger and stronger than you? When you're young, your parents, teachers and older brothers or sisters all seem so much more powerful than you are. Even when you're a teenager, adults can still seem to be the only ones who can influence and change things, which may make you wonder if it is worth even trying to make a difference.

Well, it is worth it. Even when you're young, your voice can count; your example can change other people's attitudes; your opinion does matter. It may seem to you that all the people you are expected to look up to and admire are adults, but they were once young as well. In many cases, the seeds of their greatness lay in what they did during their childhood. And there were many famous and heroic children who made their mark on history when they were young.

So who were these children and what did they do to become heroic? What does it mean to be heroic, anyway? There are many kinds of heroism. Some people are regarded as heroes because they have done something spectacularly brave; but many are heroic for other reasons. Some of the young people in this book, like musician Fanny Mendelssohn and writer Anne Frank, found themselves in situations that they would never have chosen. Their heroism lay in their courageous and creative responses to circumstances that were at odds with their natural desires and talents. Instead of becoming depressed and bitter, they found ways of flourishing and making the most of what they had. Others, like the West African ruler Sundiata and, seven centuries later, Olympic runner Wilma Rudolph, had to pit themselves against severe physical disabilities as well as extreme social conditions. Others again, like Louis IX of France, and Iqbal Masih of Pakistan, stood up to fierce opposition and threats of violence to change the values of their time. Finally, pioneers such as Helen Keller and Alexander Graham Bell stand out for their patience and persistence in working tirelessly to benefit other people.

In presenting the lives of each of these children, I have tried to tell their stories in words they might have used. I have chosen to write this way to create a better sense of what each child's world was like and what challenges it presented. History is never just a series of facts. We may know dates of battles, law reforms and other landmark events, but to understand why people behaved as they did and how they shaped their world, we need to imagine what they were like as individuals. We need to try to see things through their eyes, if only for a short while. When you turn the pages and start this book, you will travel through time to places that can only be imagined. I hope that the stories and the illustrations will make you want to find out more! If you do, you will find further books listed in the source notes. But now it is time to start. Your journey begins over half a century ago in the Netherlands, where you will meet a courageous young girl…

Rebecca Hazell

5

LIFE IN THE SECRET ANNEXE

ANNE FRANK
Holland and Germany

It is late in the evening and you're in the city of Amsterdam visiting a girl named Anne Frank. The date is 5 July 1942, the middle of the Second World War, and the German Nazis have been occupying the Netherlands for two years now. The Nazis have convinced themselves that they are a master race, and they have invaded many European countries, terrorised their peoples and taken over their wealth for themselves. The Nazis particularly hate and persecute Jews. In Holland, as elsewhere, they have passed more and more anti-Jewish laws. They have set up slave labour camps and have begun arresting Jews and sending them there. Terrifying rumours have spread that the German prison camps are nothing more than death camps for all the people they hate (which include Jews, Catholics, gypsies and intellectuals). Certainly no one ever returns from them.

Many Jews have fled the Netherlands before the arrival of the Nazis. Others have chosen to stay, thinking they will be safe in a neutral country. Anne's family have moved here from Germany, seeking safety. But since the Nazi invasion of Holland, they realise they are in terrible danger. They have just gone into hiding, in some closed-off

warehouse rooms converted by Mr Frank into a small apartment. The Franks are certain that the Allies (the British, US and Soviet troops) will defeat the Germans in the end and they hope to stay hidden here until the war is over. Some of their non-Jewish friends and employees are going to supply them with food, clothing and other items while they are in hiding. You have secretly brought them some clothing and tins of food. Because of the war, all street lights are out and blackout curtains drawn. No one should be out at night except for a good reason, and there are police and soldiers lurking nearby just waiting to arrest anyone breaking the curfew laws.

Here is Anne. She turned thirteen just a few weeks ago, and she's still half child. She has soft dark hair, green-flecked eyes and is usually bubbly and friendly with a quick smile. But her huge eyes seem sad tonight, as though they have already seen too much fear and hurt.

8

Hello: thank you for helping us. This is my — I should say our — new home until the end of the war. Surprisingly roomy for such a small space, isn't it? I hope we continue to think we have enough room, for we won't be able to leave or even betray our presence until the war is over. Except for during working hours, when a warehouseman might be expected to open a window, we'll have to keep the windows closed and heavily curtained so that no one can see inside and turn us in to the Nazis. So there's not a lot of light, either. And of course at night we put up the usual blackout curtains, but everyone has to do that, in case of air raids.

We had to disappear quickly, because the Nazis wanted to take my older sister away to a labour camp. We weren't quite ready for this big move, and in fact I knew nothing about it until the last minute. There will be seven of us. My family: Mummy and Pim (that's my father), and my sister Margot. Then there's Pim's business partner, Herr van Pels, his wife and their son, Peter. They'll be joining us shortly.

Only up past Peter's room, in the topmost attic, can we dare open the skylight for fresh air. We're going to have to be so careful to stay quiet, and keep lights from being seen from the outside. Everything from cooking to bathing is going to be a challenge in this tiny space. And we don't know how successful our friends will be at getting supplies to us. After all, they're suffering from the war shortages as well. Everyone's supplies are rationed, because the Germans are seizing basic things like coal, cheese and meat and taking them back to Germany.

I'm trying to look upon this time as a great adventure but, to tell the truth, we're all really scared. We've heard the tales about slave camps, and we don't want to find out if they're true!

It's strange to think that a short while ago, we had such a lovely life. We were well off and had many friends — especially me. I was always surrounded by girlfriends, and boyfriends too. Some of the boys were in love with me, I think. (Now there will only be that Peter van Pels. He's too quiet and reserved for me, plus he's a couple of years older than I am, so goodbye to romance.) I was crazy about movie stars — actually I still am.

Look at the photos I've been saving. Pim remembered to bring them with us. I'm decorating my walls with them. While we're here I'll be taking lessons to keep up with my school work, and I suppose I'll have plenty of time to read now. We'll mostly have to get the news from our friends. Jews aren't allowed to have radios any more. I suppose we can sneak downstairs into the office after hours and listen to the radio there occasionally.

I just celebrated my birthday recently and got all sorts of presents, but my favourite one is this diary. I've started writing in it regularly, and now I'm going to keep a journal of life in the Secret Annexe. That's what I've decided to call our hiding place here. My diary is going to be my best friend. I know that already. I'd like to be a famous author some day, when we get back to normal.

9

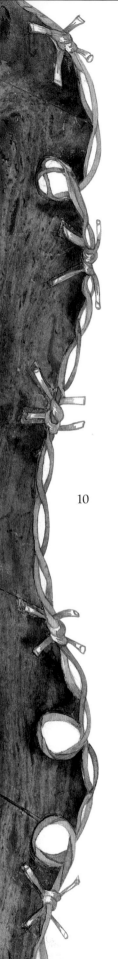

10

One of the first things I'll write about is what it's like living under Nazi occupation. Bit by bit since they invaded, the government of occupation has been passing laws that restrict our freedom. For instance, Jews can't own businesses now, so Pim had to hand his business over to his Christian partners, and then be paid on the sly. We've been taken out of normal school and made to go to schools for Jewish children only. Many of my old friends had to stop playing with me. We had to start wearing a yellow Star of David on our clothing to distinguish us from everyone else. Jews can't ride in trams, so those Jews who still have work, like Pim, have to walk miles to their jobs. We even had to hand in our bicycles. We can only shop in certain shops, at certain times of day, and can't sit in our own gardens in the evenings. We can't go to the cinema or swim or play sports.

They're making Jews who live in the countryside move into Amsterdam. They just have to pack up and leave, with nowhere to go! The worst has been the pogroms — group riots against Jews — beatings, the burning of Jewish homes and businesses, and the sudden arrests and disappearances. The Nazis have started making surprise raids and arresting people. We hear they're being shipped east to do slave labour.

But I'm young and cheerful. I can always look around and find something good in the world around me, whether it's tasting cold sweet ice-cream or simply gazing at the bright blue of the sky. I'm grateful, too, that so many Dutch people sympathise with us and try to help us in secret. They could go to prison or be put to death for aiding a Jew! I think they're very brave. As for me, I think it's very important right now to behave cheerfully for the sake of other people, even when I don't feel that way inside. That's why I know my diary is going to be very important to me. I'm going to tell it everything about how I feel: how Mummy still treats me like a little child and how Pim is my favourite parent. What we eat and what I read, and just everything I think of. Will I let you read it? Well...maybe. Someday.

What happened to Anne? She and her people hid for two long, dangerous years. Another man joined them, and Anne had to share a room with him. She thought he was stuffy, and they did not get on. She fell in and out of love with shy, quiet Peter.

Anne did make her diary into her best friend. She wrote about life in hiding, her loves and hates, and about how hard life was, with the adults bickering over small things, and Peter retreating into a shell. She told of no privacy, of bad or no food and little fresh air, of finding small ways to enjoy life. As she grew older, her story became that of every young girl growing up — except that she lived in constant fear of discovery and death.

Just before the end of the war, someone (no one knows who) betrayed Anne's group to the Nazis. They were among the last Jews arrested before the Allies freed the Netherlands. They were first sent to a death camp, Auschwitz, where the men and women were separated. There Anne saw long lines of children enter gas chambers to be killed. Then Mrs Frank died, and Anne and her sister were sent to a labour camp. Here they both fell ill with a deadly disease, typhus, and died a month before their camp was freed by the Allies. Mr Frank alone survived. All the others were among the ten million people who died at the hands of the Nazis. Of these, over six million were Jews, over one and a half million of whom were children. This epic tragedy is known today as the Holocaust.

When Mr Frank returned to Amsterdam, he found that the woman who had helped hide his family had secretly saved Anne's diary. Knowing the war was almost over, Anne had been rewriting it, hoping it would be published. Her father continued her work and the diary was published in 1947. Its voice of hope in the midst of hopelessness has pierced people's hearts ever since.

Twenty days before her arrest, Anne wrote, 'It's really a wonder I haven't dropped all my ideals...Yet in spite of everything I still believe that people are really good at heart.' Anne's diary has been published in over fifty-five languages. After the Bible, it is the most widely read book in the world.

11

THE HUNGERING LION

SUNDIATA
West Africa

You have just travelled many miles and many years further back in time, to West Africa, around the year 1220. You are walking along a dusty, well-trodden path. Walking near you are a sturdy boy of ten or eleven, his hunchbacked mother, his brothers and sisters, a few servants, and a large caravan of merchants and porters. The sun beats down like a mallet. Flies and mosquitoes zoom around you, eager to bite.

Your group trudges across the vast plain, composed of miles and miles of short grasses, dotted with baobab trees. This is the great African savannah south of the Sahara Desert.

Unfamiliar birds fly overhead and in the distance you see trees marking the path of a river and a village tucked among the trees. The little thatch-topped conical huts line up neatly near the river bank. Some men and boys are herding long-horned buffalo nearby and they shout a greeting to your group. Behind you black porters bear loads on their heads or lead heavily laden donkeys through the yellow grasses and past the huge, many-trunked baobab trees.

The merchants are mostly foreign, Muslim traders from North Africa. They risk the dangerous journey across the great Sahara Desert to trade with the

tribes and nations here in what is called the Sudan, and to bring the religion of Islam to them. They wear turbans and simple robes, while the local people like the boy and his mother wear colourful cotton clothing, heavily embroidered, or, in some cases, they are clad in very little at all. The boy wears a turban, as he is a Muslim. He and his family are all adorned with massive ornaments of solid gold. Gold is plentiful in this part of the world. It is like a magnet that draws traders across the Sahara, despite the risks of being lost in the vast, waterless desert.

The boy you are walking with is named Mari Djata, or Sundiata, the 'Hungering Lion', as he will become known to future generations. He and his family are on a journey from their home village of Niani, fleeing under the protection of the merchants. They hope to find refuge with the king of another village, somewhere to rest in safety from the threat of death that follows them.

'Why does someone want to kill you?' you ask Sundiata.

*B*ecause there is a prophecy about me. This great prophecy began with my mother, Sogolon, who was given to my father by two mysterious hunters as he held court under the great baobab tree outside our village. My father was Naré Maghan, the Lion-King of Niani in Mali, the eternal land. With my father was his griot* — the wise bard who holds the truth of the past and the secrets of the future in his song, who advises kings and casts spells with his music. Father's griot told him that this strange woman would be the mother of his successor, even though she was so ugly and my father so handsome. Father married her anyway, and Sogolon became his favourite wife. This angered his first wife, the beautiful Sassouma Bérété, who feared that her own son Dankaran Touman would no

longer become king when my father died. She knew the choice always rested in my father's hands.

But when I was born, her fears faded. Even though a great storm announced my arrival — a good omen — I was weak and sickly. I could barely talk as I grew older, and I could not walk at all. I had to pull myself about with my arms because my legs were useless. All I wanted to do was eat. My father's other children made fun of me and my ugly mother, and my father almost lost hope for me. Just the same, when I was seven, he gave me my own griot, the son of his griot. His name is Bella Fasséké, and he is the living history of my people. His task is to teach me how to become a great and wise king, and to recite the great deeds of the past and remind me of the truth of

*pronounced *gree-oh*

14

the present. He taught me about the great emperors, even the mighty Alexander the Great from the far north beyond the desert of sand and salt oases.

Then my father died and we were left alone. My father's eldest son became king instead of me, and because my body was crippled and weak, I thought there was nothing I could do about it. The new king's mother, that scheming Sassouma Bérété, was the real ruler, though. And the person who ruled her was Sumanguru — the evil sorcerer-king

I got the smith — who has the power to transform iron into weapons — to make me a long thick iron staff. Holding on to it, I slowly and painfully pulled myself up until I could stand. Indeed, my strength was so great that I bent the thick rod like a bow! My griot, Bella Fasséké, celebrated my achievement with a special song which he called 'Hymn to the Bow'.

who invades one small kingdom after another to add it to his empire, which he controls through witchcraft. Sassouma Bérété sent my mother and me to live in a poor hut in the back yard of the palace and we were treated badly by everyone. When one day my mother ran to our hut weeping at their cruel mockery, I finally made up my mind. I would walk. I must walk!

After that, I slowly and painfully learned to walk, and then to hunt. I learned to hunt the lion and the panther, the gazelle and the antelope, to prove my manhood and to provide meat for the village. At last I was initiated into the hunter-warrior society and soon had my own friends and followers, some of them the princely sons of other chiefs who had been raised by my father. My elder

16

half-brother and his mother grew ever more jealous and afraid. Sassouma Bérété was especially fearful and tried to kill us through witchcraft. She paid five witches to destroy me, but I won them over with kindness and they let me be. Even so, my mother decided to take us away from Niani.

But before we could leave, Sassouma Bérété did cause me harm. She got her son to steal Bella Fasséké from me and sent him and one of her daughters to the court of Sumanguru to keep peace with him. My griot became Niani's ambassador and my poor half-sister became the magician-king's bride.

Imagine my anger! I stood up to my elder half-brother and warned him: I was leaving for now, but I would return triumphant. I am only a boy today, but I know that a great destiny awaits me. Everything that happens is the will of Allah, who foresees and prepares the way. In Him I put my trust.

Now we seek the protection of another king, but Sassouma Bérété's ill-will follows us everywhere. She tried to bribe one king to kill me, and threatened war with another if he gave me shelter. Then we tried Wagadou, once the capital of the old empire of Ghana. Sumanguru has conquered what is left of Ghana. He is pure evil. He treats everyone he has conquered like slaves. He takes their wealth, abuses their women and kills people for sport. I will destroy him one day. This I know, even without Bella Fasséké by my side to counsel me. And I must have my griot back!

Now we travel to faraway Mema. We hope to find shelter there. We are told that its king is a good man and a tribal cousin. Surely he will take us in?

After many weeks, Sundiata and his mother arrived with their followers in Mema, where they were greeted as honoured guests and allowed to stay.

Over the next few years, Sundiata grew into a great hunter and leader of men. The King of Mema came to trust him and trained him to become a mighty warrior. In fact, having no children of his own, he planned to make Sundiata his heir. By the time Sundiata was eighteen, he was already Viceroy of Mema.

But Sundiata's destiny led elsewhere. As a devout Muslim, he would have said that his fate had been decided from birth and nothing could change it.

While Sundiata was away in exile, Mali had been completely overrun by Sumanguru, the magician-king. He captured the town of Niani and burned it to ashes. The survivors fled. Some say that the people of Mali then began a great search to find Sundiata, the rightful king, to lead a rebellion against the evil Sumanguru. Others say that Sumanguru's unhappy subjects were drawn to Sundiata's growing fame as a warrior and leader.

According to one story, people searched all over the Sudan for him, and finally tracked him down in Mema. Sundiata's mother had died, and the King of Mema reluctantly let him leave so that he could fight Sumanguru. Sundiata's skill as a general and a warrior drew more and more support from other rebel leaders. In 1230 they proclaimed him King of Mali, and afterwards, in a series of thrilling battles, he put Sumanguru on the defensive. However, because of the magician-king's sorcery, the young hero could never get close enough to capture or kill him.

Finally, in the year 1235, Sundiata's destiny was fulfilled. First, his half-sister, who had been forced to marry Sumanguru, and then his faithful griot, Bella Fasséké, managed to escape the magician's clutches and made their way to Sundiata. Bella Fasséké had secretly visited the sorcerer's private tower, where he kept his magic and his totem. He described to the young hero what he had seen: 'The walls were lined with human skins and on them hung strange and terrible weapons. There was a mat of human skin on the floor where Sumanguru sat when he came to the chamber to cast spells. It was full of fetishes: a monstrous snake, guardian owls that could speak, and the skulls of nine great kings he had slain.'

17

But it was Sundiata's half-sister who had found a way to break the sorcerer's power, by flattering her husband and praising his strength. He boasted to her that iron could not harm him. Only the touch of the spur of a cockerel's claw could break the deep spells that protected him.

At the next battle, instead of his usual bow and arrows, Sundiata carried a special arrow, made of wood only and with no iron tip. Instead, he tipped the arrow with the poisoned spur of a white cockerel. He and his men threw themselves on the enemy, but as soon as Sundiata saw Sumanguru, he took aim and shot the special arrow with his mighty bow. It only grazed the sorcerer-king, but that was enough. Sumanguru's power was broken.

Different griots tell the rest of the story in different ways. Some say that the evil king vanished instantly. Others claim he called on his last bit of power and turned into a baobab tree — or a mountain. And others claim that Sundiata chased him into a mountain only to find that the sorcerer had disappeared.

18

Instead, the young warrior came upon an enchanted pool that he drank from and which gave him magical powers.

Whichever story you choose to believe, this much is known: Sundiata was acclaimed by all the kings and princes whose lands Sumanguru had conquered — he became the new ruler of the new empire: Mali, the eternal land. For several years, he continued to make further conquests. By then, it was mostly his many royal generals who commanded his army, for by 1240 he no longer led men into battle, because he was busy establishing a safe and just kingdom for all his people to share. Muslim and pagan alike found that they could lead peaceful lives, fulfilling their own destinies as merchants or artisans, warriors or hunters, fishermen or herdsmen. Sundiata died in 1255, the first great emperor of the great empire of Mali. He is remembered in history as the saviour of his people, the Son of the Lion of Mali.

COMPOSER IN WAITING

FANNY MENDELSSOHN
Germany

You are leaping forward in time now, to the year 1820. You are visiting a young lady in Berlin, the capital of an empire that will one day become the nation of Germany. You find yourself in a pleasant house that stands in a wealthy neighbourhood. The elegant room you are entering looks out on to a garden of bright flowers. The room itself is tastefully furnished, with sofas and chairs, books tucked into cases, figurines on little tables, walls lined with pictures.

Seated at a piano near the window are a girl of sixteen and a boy of twelve. They are performing a duet, not only with their music but with the affectionate glances they send each other. Their dark curls almost mingle sometimes, their fingers fly across the keyboard, their voices soar together as they sway with delight to the music. You listen quietly. The girl's voice is especially sweet. In it you can almost hear birds singing and feel the warmth of the summer sun.

This pair of children are no ordinary musicians. They are the two eldest Mendelssohn children, and the music they are playing is a piece they composed together for their own entertainment. The boy, Felix, is already being compared to the child prodigy Mozart, who died about thirty years before. The girl, Fanny, is just as talented.

As the duet ends, one of the children's tutors calls to Felix, and after cheerfully smiling and shaking hands with you, he darts out of the room. Fanny also shakes hands with you and leads you to a stiff, uncomfortable-looking sofa.

A servant brings in a tea tray and you watch Fanny as she gracefully pours cups of tea for the two of you. She is a serious girl with a quick, quiet way of doing things. She is not beautiful, though she has large dark eyes and reveals perfect teeth when she smiles. Her left shoulder is hunched a little higher than her right one, but she dresses so nicely that you barely notice. You sit drinking fragrant tea out of delicate china cups (and munching on delicious butter cake) as Fanny tells you her story.

I'm very pleased to meet you. Did you enjoy our little song? I love music, both playing and composing it.

My life is very fortunate. My grandfather, Moses Mendelssohn, was once a poverty-stricken boy from an isolated Jewish ghetto, but he changed not only our lives but the lives of all Jews in Europe. He lived from hand to mouth, but he educated himself, and became a successful author and businessman. Even the Emperor admired him. My grandfather crusaded to break down the barriers of the ghettos. Because of him, several European countries lifted the worst restrictions against Jews. Nowadays Jews are true citizens and can get a decent education and enter society. By the time Father was born, our family was rich, not because we have money,

but because we value learning and art and truth.

I remind myself of this when Father wakens us for lessons at five o'clock in the morning. It's hard to be grateful then! I love Sundays — we get to sleep in until seven! Of course, we are now officially Christian. Despite all that Grandfather achieved, many people — especially Germans — still hate and fear Jews. When other children called Felix and me names, threw rocks and spat on us, my parents decided that they did not want us to be martyrs. So, when I was eleven, we were baptised. We go to church every Sunday, and feel we belong to two great traditions now.

And I am truly grateful for my wonderful education. We have travelled, and we don't go to school like other

22

children. Instead we have tutors, not only for academic subjects like Latin, Greek and history, but for sports and art and music. And Father and Mother often invite their famous friends to visit, like the explorer and scientist Alexander Humboldt and the poet Heinrich Heine. They have big parties with lots of discussions and music and laughter. Sometimes we children put on Shakespeare's plays, or Felix and I play music, which I enjoy the most.

When I was born, my mother claimed I had fingers made for playing Bach fugues. When I was thirteen, I could already play all thirty-four of his fugues from memory. Oh, Johann Sebastian Bach was one of the greatest German composers of the last century. He is one of our heroes, but he's been nearly forgotten. Felix and I agree that when he becomes famous, he will remind people about our neglected hero. Of course, he is not going to be merely a famous, but a great musician and composer. You see, Father insists that Felix must prove himself or he will have to go into business instead.

But I will never be a musician. Father forbids it. He says that, for me, music must always be a 'decoration'. My role in life is to become a wife and mother, to serve my husband and children at home with my education and talents. I must play music well, so that the family can enjoy it.

It breaks my heart. I know that if I had the chance, I could be by Felix's side. Yet I have to accept Father's commands. He is strict but I love and respect him. So I will marry and have children. (I've already met someone special, but don't tell anyone!) On the outside, I will obey. But I refuse to give up my dreams. If I cannot publish or perform my music, I will help Felix. He and I are almost like twins. I call him our soul. We have our own secret language, and we love to play pranks on each other. Since we were small, I've been helping him compose. He shows me everything he writes, and he won't play anything until I've approved it. He plays my music, too.

Now that he's performing, he tries to credit my work when he can, or he slips my music into his compositions. Why, when he visited the great German author Johann Goethe, he played one of my songs for him. Herr Goethe even sent me a thank-you poem. I'll treasure it forever. And I am invited to meet him, too.

Am I jealous of Felix? No, I love him, and he deserves to be famous. He is a genius. And something else, too, a truly kind and decent boy. Yet I do wish that some day I could publish my pieces under my own name…

23

anny was right. Her brother, Felix Mendelssohn, did become a famous composer, conductor and musician, a 'superstar' of his day. He travelled all over Europe, and when he arrived in a city, people flocked from miles around to hear him conduct and perform, sleeping in fields when the hotels were full. (Today people still fall under the spell of works like *A Midsummer Night's Dream*, based on Shakespeare's play, or *Fingal's Cave*.) Felix reintroduced audiences to the music of his and Fanny's forgotten hero, Johann Sebastian Bach, and Fanny was present at his first performance of Bach's *St Matthew Passion*, singing in the chorus.

In England, he charmed society both with his music and with his kindness and wit. Young Queen Victoria and Prince Albert even invited him to play for them. On his visit, the queen picked out one of her best-loved pieces for Felix to play while she sang. It was a song written by Fanny.

Throughout this time, Fanny stayed dutifully at home. Felix continued to share his musical ideas with her: she still had to give final approval. She rejoiced at his success, sending him his favourite cakes along with musical suggestions — and copies of her own music. Some of these her brother published under his own name, and others he wove into his own music. In this way she was able to see her work published, and had the satisfaction of knowing that Felix would credit her work when he could, and boast about her talent as a pianist, too.

When she was fifteen, Fanny had met a promising young artist, Wilhelm Hensel. He proposed when she was seventeen, but her mother sent him away to test their affection for each other. Her sweetheart courted her from afar for five years, through her mother. He sent Mrs Mendelssohn sketch after sketch of Fanny, Felix, and the other family members, all done from memory, to show how serious he was about Fanny. Finally they were allowed to marry. But Wilhelm always had to share Fanny's love because Felix and his music were never far from her mind. In the same way, Felix's wife always had to make room for his loyalty to Fanny.

24

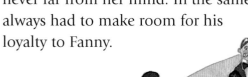

Fanny and her husband and only son lived in a house on a huge property purchased by the Mendelssohns. Just as her parents had done, she hosted weekly concerts, social events where a winning combination of music, conversation and food drew the most talented and interesting people in Europe to her doors. If she could not go out, the world must be invited in.

Through letters to Fanny, Felix shared his friendships with other musical stars: Robert Schumann, Franz Liszt, Frederick Chopin and Hector Berlioz. She even met and became friends with some of them. Whenever Felix came home to visit, Fanny arranged concerts for him, either at home or in churches and concert halls, where hordes of Berliners always rushed to see him.

After her father died, Fanny got to travel again. Even happier for her, she finally published some of her songs under her own name. Her 'album' was a success, and perhaps she would have published more. Though she had said for years that there was no point in writing songs that would never be sung, she had written over four hundred pieces of music. Had she been encouraged to publish and perform herself, she might well have written more.

Shortly after her publishing success, when Fanny was only forty-one, she died suddenly of a stroke while she was sitting at the piano. When Felix received the news, he collapsed. For years he had been pushing too hard to conduct, perform and produce more music. Without Fanny, his joy in life died. Within a few months, he too died almost as suddenly as she had. It is almost as if one 'soul' had lived inside two people.

25

Today Fanny is receiving more of the musical attention she deserves. Had she been given the same encouragement and training as Felix, perhaps today we would be listening to the famous works of two musical Mendelssohns. Instead, when we listen to Felix's music, we must be content with catching little echoes in it — the traces of Fanny's song.

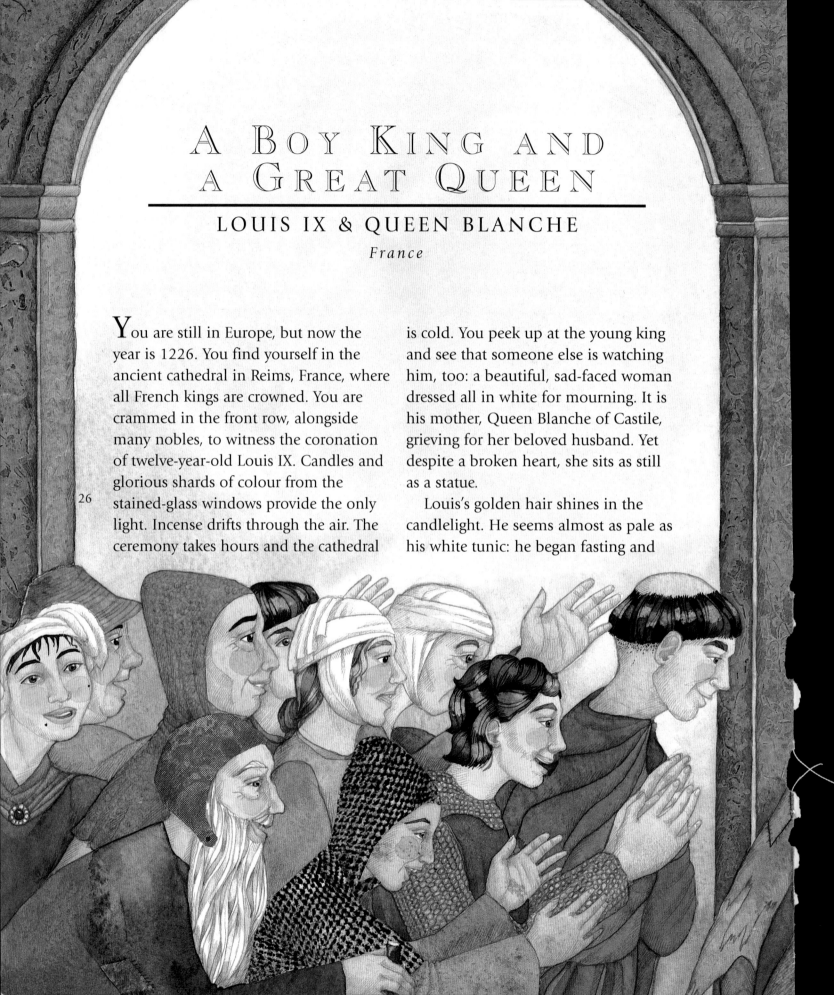

A Boy King and a Great Queen

LOUIS IX & QUEEN BLANCHE

France

You are still in Europe, but now the year is 1226. You find yourself in the ancient cathedral in Reims, France, where all French kings are crowned. You are crammed in the front row, alongside many nobles, to witness the coronation of twelve-year-old Louis IX. Candles and glorious shards of colour from the stained-glass windows provide the only light. Incense drifts through the air. The ceremony takes hours and the cathedral is cold. You peek up at the young king and see that someone else is watching him, too: a beautiful, sad-faced woman dressed all in white for mourning. It is his mother, Queen Blanche of Castile, grieving for her beloved husband. Yet despite a broken heart, she sits as still as a statue.

Louis's golden hair shines in the candlelight. He seems almost as pale as his white tunic: he began fasting and

26

praying at dawn. The bishop has already anointed him with holy oil, and now comes the robing ceremony. The young king dons the same coronation garments worn 450 years earlier by the mighty emperor Charlemagne, a giant of a man. Select nobles help the bishop robe the king in a long embroidered over-garment and a mantle trimmed with ermine. He receives blue slippers with golden spurs and a sheathed sword to wear. He puts on a special ring and takes a sceptre in each hand. Everything is too big for him. The bishop and nobles place the jewelled crown of Charlemagne on Louis's head. It threatens to slip over his eyes, it is so big. Last, he is shown the massive sword of Charlemagne. Louis's poise and dignity never waver.

Now you are outside with the crowds of cheering people waiting for their new king as he leaves the church. He strides by, wearing his own clothing again — royal scarlet — surrounded by his nobles. He stops suddenly in front of a group of ragged beggars. They are not begging, only hoping to see their new king. One is a leper who must avoid other people because his disease is contagious. To everyone's astonishment, King Louis stoops and kisses the leper's hand, ordering that the man receive extra alms from the royal treasury on this special day. Then he moves on.

That night, you visit King Louis for a few minutes. Entering his private chamber, you glimpse him on his knees, praying in front of a crucifix. He gets up and sits down in the only chair in the room. You bow courteously and stand respectfully as he tells his story. He is exhausted after all the ceremonies and celebrations, but his blue eyes sparkle with excitement.

28

Welcome. My heart is almost too full today. It overflows with sadness because my father has just died. I did not know him very well, but I am sure he would have been a great king had he lived longer. He was often away from home fighting for France. Of course, my poor mother's heart is broken. She and Father loved each other deeply, unlike many couples in arranged marriages. They were always in agreement. For instance, they agreed that I should be raised as both a good Christian and a brave warrior. Some day I hope to be a good Christian warrior fighting real battles.

Yet my heart also flows with gladness because I saw today that already the people of France wish me well. Did you see how they thronged the streets to see me, and how they cheered? They were shocked when I kissed the leper's hand. But Christ healed ten lepers, and it was a sign from God that ten beggars were waiting to see me. Even if I can't heal like Christ, at least I can honour the sick and needy as He would have us all do.

As Mother says, I belong to the people of France now, no longer to myself. To me, that means all the people of France, not just the rich and nobly born. I think too many of my nobles care only for their own power and position. We're having trouble with some of the most powerful of them already — they weren't there today. They are angry that I'm only twelve and that my mother will be my regent until I'm old enough to rule by myself. They say she is only a woman, and a foreigner, because she is part Spanish. They want to put my uncle on the throne. Let them try! I think the people of France may object.

Mother and I expect to face many different struggles over the next few years, but we're prepared. We've inherited feuds with other kings — like with King Henry III of England. It's a shame, since we're kin, but if there's a war between England and France, I want to lead it.

You know, the reason my father and mother were married was to stop the quarrels between England and France. Now, there is a story for you: the story of my mother, Queen Blanche, and how she came to marry my father. Let me tell you in the way that she told me.

She was born in Castile, in the sunny land of Spain, the youngest of three sisters. Her father was the King of Castile, and her mother was the daughter of King Henry II of England and Queen Eleanor, Duchess of Aquitaine, which is one of the greatest duchies of France.

Like mine, her childhood was short, and spent learning two things. The first was to love and fear God. The second was to prepare to marry a king or noble who would be a good ally for her family. Even when she was small, she had to behave like a future queen.

Her eldest sister was already married when Mother and her sister Urraca were

called to the court one day. There they found a group of ambassadors standing about speaking in a foreign language. Seated next to their mother was a lady who was very old but so regal-looking that one knew she was a queen.

Mother and Urraca were introduced to their grandmother, Queen Eleanor of Aquitaine, still the most powerful woman in Europe. They spoke of small things, but Mother could tell the queen was inspecting them both. It could only mean that she was looking for a bride. Later, my mother found out that this was indeed her intent: a bride for the future King of France. It was to bring peace between France and England, so her choice was very important.

Urraca was older and prettier than Mother, so they were both surprised when, after a few days, Mother was summoned to meet with her grandmother. Queen Eleanor announced that my mother had been chosen for this important role. She had seen something special in her. Mother was to leave with her right away although it was winter and cold even in Spain.

Bidding a sad farewell to her family, knowing they would never meet again, she and the old queen crossed the Pyrenees — the mountain range between Spain and France — in the

mother could dare to hope for more. She could become a helpmeet and adviser to her husband if she showed him that she was loyal and wise. Mother took her advice to heart.

When they arrived in Paris, my mother became the wife of Prince Louis, the Dauphin of France, in the year of our Lord 1200. She was only eleven, even younger than I am. In time she stopped missing her home in Spain. In spirit she became French. She put God, France and its people before everything else.

I think Mother was lucky. She and Father grew to love and trust one another, and he never treated her the

dead of winter. Imagine! It was cold and dangerous, even with the protection of the vast army of knights and servants that went with them. They had to face winter snow storms and treacherous passes, not to mention possible bandit attacks. Once over the mountains they hurried north, through the rich lands belonging to Queen Eleanor. The queen was already seventy-nine years old and getting tired. Almost no one lives to that age!

Throughout their journey, her grandmother taught Mother how to be a good wife and queen. The most important lesson she learned was that she now belonged to France. Mother says that Queen Eleanor gave her some unusual advice, too. As a wife she should regard her husband as her master. But because Eleanor had never been obedient when she was young, she added that my

30

way many husbands treat their wives. Especially the way many kings treat their queens — as only a source of property and of sons. She gave Father five sons, including me, and he respected her advice and good judgement. Long ago he wrote in his will that she should be my guardian and regent in case of his early death.

Alas, we needed that will. Father had been king for only four years when suddenly he died. On receiving the news, Mother fainted. Some say that, in a frenzy of grief, she even tried to kill herself. I don't know about that. I do know that she has had to oversee my coronation even though it's been only three weeks since Father died. But France comes before her own feelings. I had to be crowned quickly before certain disloyal nobles rebelled. We still may have to fight them.

Mother agrees that I should lead my own armies. She's as brave as a man, and she knows I must show leadership right away. I admire and love her, even though she is so strict with her children. She has been especially strict with me as the Dauphin, since I always had to be ready for kingship. Life is dangerous and sometimes short, even for a king. That's why I was raised the way I was. She watched over my education carefully.

I've been trained as a knight, to lead men and fight bravely. I love swordplay and jousting. I practise as often as I can. I love hunting and falconry, too, but Mother discourages me from pursuing frivolous pastimes.

She also made sure I was educated by the wisest and most learned men of the Church. I can even read and write! And I've learned to devote myself to God and his children, my people, just as she has. I try to deal fairly and truthfully at all costs. Few enough do these days. I try to avoid all sin. Mother says she would rather I died than commit a mortal sin! And I try to pray to God constantly for his blessings on all our people and forgiveness for all our sins.

I have a secret ambition, though. While I must always serve France, I hope some day to see it wealthy and peaceful enough for me to join a crusade. I want to liberate Jerusalem and the Holy Land from the Saracen infidels forever! The kings of Europe have been trying for 200 years but, after their first success, they've been slowly driven back to a few little kingdoms. Worst of all, Jerusalem is back in Saracen hands. We must take it back! Think of it: to win glory, or to die in God's cause. The Pope promises Paradise for those who die thus. Now that would be the greatest adventure of all…

What happened to Louis and his mother? He was right about his people. After his coronation, having just sworn allegiance to him, renegade nobles tried to kidnap him and Queen Blanche as they rode home to his capital city, Paris. However, his supporters alerted the citizens of Paris and the common people swarmed out to where he was trapped, lining the road to protect him, and singing hymns as he passed between them to safety.

Afterwards Blanche and Louis led an army against the English-supported rebel nobles. They were a dramatic sight, she dressed in white from head to toe and riding a white stallion, and he decked out in armour and a scarlet cloak. They did not need to fight. The English army never arrived and the nobles had to surrender. Instead of executing them, Louis and his mother behaved with such mercy that soon even they were won over.

Over the years, despite troubles with their own nobles and with other nations, Louis and Queen Blanche ruled France so well that its people began to think of themselves as part of one kingdom instead of a hotchpotch of baronies, duchies and counties. France became the wealthiest and most powerful kingdom in Europe. King Louis relied heavily on his mother's advice to the end of her life. She even chose a bride for him, and they in turn fell in love. Queen Margaret was a good queen, but could never compete with the strong character of her mother-in-law.

32

Louis developed a reputation for saintliness. He built churches, monasteries, convents and hospitals, sometimes helping with his own hands. He gave alms to the poor and sick, not from a distance, but in person, and he made laws that protected the weak. He was so respected that even enemy kings asked for him to judge their disputes with each other. He was known as a man who put truth before his own gain, a quality still rare today. He lived simply in an era of gaudiness and greed. And he radiated a sweetness and courage that won over even the hardest-hearted warriors.

Louis was able to fulfil his dream of going on a crusade to the Holy Land, not once but twice. He felt honour bound to do so, because in 1244 he had nearly died of a fever, and had vowed to become a crusader if he recovered.

Though this was a time when Christians and Muslims both behaved with unimaginable cruelty towards each other, inflicting war, plague and starvation on the Holy Land, Europeans thought of the Crusades as a holy mission.

Both of Louis's crusades failed. The first time, from 1248–51, he left his mother to govern France, confident that it was safe in her hands. However, he was captured and held for ransom in Egypt by his Muslim enemies. Only his courage and self-possession saved him from death at their hands. Queen Blanche personally gathered much of the huge ransom needed to buy his freedom. She died shortly before he returned home, of a heart ailment. Perhaps her broken heart had never healed. Louis now had to rule alone, his health ruined by war and illness.

Louis tried to lead a second crusade in 1270, but he was now an old man, growing weaker daily. He fell mortally ill, but died happy, confident that his efforts had won him entry into Paradise. After his passing, there were no more great crusades. But his memory did not fade. The people of France loved him so much that they made his tomb into a shrine. Within a few years, stories of miraculous healing at King Louis's tomb spread across the kingdom. By 1297 Louis IX had been declared a saint by the Roman Catholic Church. In France he is still revered as a great king and a great man. But once he was only a boy who learned from his mother how to serve his God and his people.

FROM SORCERER TO SAINT

MILAREPA
Tibet

You have just taken another leap in time and space, all the way to medieval Tibet, in Central Asia. It is the year 1057, or thereabouts. You are standing in a valley bare of trees, wedged in by snow-crowned mountains. Green fields of barley wave in the constant wind, but the mountains are stark and barren. They seem to be pushing the sky up, they are so high. The sun shines as though it would melt you, but the breeze coming off the mountains carries the chill of snow. You see a few stone houses in the distance, decorated with bright-red pillars, and a few hairy yaks, horses and woolly sheep grazing here and there,

tended by a couple of shepherds. A handful of other people are working in the fields but, except for them, the valley seems empty and even lonely.

Near you, a boy no older than seventeen is building what looks like a tower. Stripped to the waist, he is carrying such a heavy boulder on his back that he staggers under its weight. As you approach him, you see that he is a handsome youth, with long blue-black hair, shiny red cheeks and almond-shaped eyes. He is singing to himself, and his melodious voice seems to draw you towards him. One day he will be known as Milarepa, 'the Cotton-Clad', the most

famous Buddhist saint in Tibet, but he
doesn't know that yet. His given name is
'Good News'.

He carries the boulder up a rickety-
looking ladder and drops it into place,
then climbs back down to greet you.
Wiping the sweat off his face, he cheerily
invites you to share a small meal with
him: a bit of dried meat and some tsampa
— barley flour mixed with butter. You
hunker down next to the tower wall, out
of the wind, and he agrees to tell you
why he is building it.

35

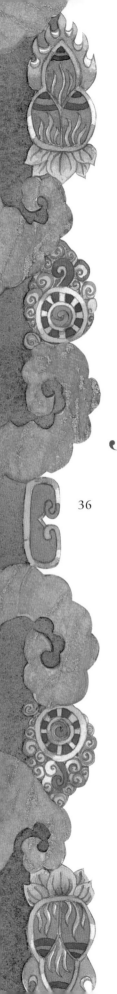

36

I am building this tower for Marpa the Translator, the master of these lands. He is a great, enlightened teacher who went to India to bring back the teachings of the Lord Buddha. He has told me that if I build him this tower, he will accept me as a student and teach me the holy Dharma, the path that the Buddha taught. I need to study and practise it as much as I can, because I have stained my being with black deeds and now I must learn how to purify myself of them.

What did I do? Oh, I must begin at the beginning for you to understand. My father was a prosperous merchant and I was his first child. That is why he named me Good News. I was raised gently and with love, but when I was only seven, my father became sick and died.

Before his death, he made his will and asked his brother and sister-in-law to look after my mother and little sister and me until I grew up.

But after the funeral, my uncle and his wife turned against us and stole our wealth. They made the three of us into their servants and treated us harshly. Instead of ornaments of turquoise, coral and silver, we were forced to dress in rags and to work like beasts, summer and winter. Our food was fit only for dogs and our tasks were suited only for donkeys. My mother, who is strong in her love for her friends and in hatred for her enemies, grew bitter as the years passed. It broke my heart to see my beloved mother and my beautiful little sister turned into wretched beings, pale and thin as skeletons.

When I turned fifteen, she tried one last time to force her brother-in-law to restore our wealth to us. Her brother had saved up enough money for her to buy meat and make barley bread and beer. With these, she made a feast and invited our relatives, the girl I loved and my aunt and uncle, to it. She told everyone there that it was time for us to have our own home and wealth back, now that I was almost grown and hoping to marry.

But my wicked aunt and uncle refused, claiming that everything my father had owned had actually belonged to his brother, and that my father had possessed nothing. Therefore there was no wealth to give back! They claimed that my mother must be wealthy enough already if she could afford to put on such a feast. They struck her and threatened to turn us out into the world as beggars. They said that we could fight them if we dared. If not, we could try magic spells. Then they swept from the feast, leaving us weeping bitterly at their cruel taunts.

Somehow after that we managed to eke out a living with help from our friends and relatives, and by working for others. But we were not happy. My mother could not even bear to see happiness in others. One day she over-heard me singing, and she went almost mad with rage and grief. In my regret for

making her even more unhappy, I agreed to do anything she asked me.

All she wanted was revenge on her cruel brother-in-law and his greedy wife. And the only way she could think of getting it was to follow her brother-in-law's own advice: to cast a curse on them. Selling some of the little plot of land her brother kept for her, she used the money to send me to a black magician who practises the old religion of Tibet, Bön. She warned me before I left to study with him that, if I did not succeed in getting revenge on our relatives, she would kill herself before my very eyes. We parted with many tears.

Spurred on by my mother's dire threat, I learned the arts of casting curses and spells in only fourteen days. With my black magic, I caused my uncle's house to collapse during the wedding feast of his son. His horses kicked the walls down and thirty-five of our enemies died. Only my aunt and uncle survived, so that they could know suffering and loss, just as we had known it.

My mother rejoiced loudly when she heard the news, making our neighbours in the village fear what might happen to them. Her old enemies were dead, but now she had new enemies. Her brother warned her that the remaining villagers wanted to kill both of us, me first and

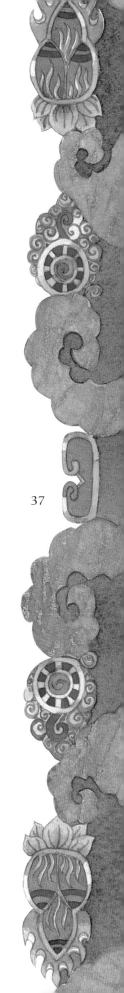

37

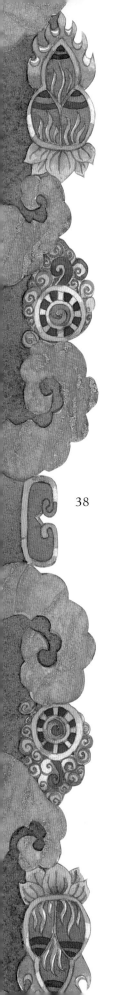

then her. She sent me a secret message demanding that I destroy the crops in the village to make the villagers so afraid of me that they would never threaten either of us again. I had to obey my beloved mother, so I called down a terrible hailstorm that destroyed all the crops just at harvest time. Now everyone hated and feared us.

Seeing that nothing but misery had been gained, I was filled with remorse for the evil I had done. All I could think of now was how to make amends. I began to long for the teachings of the Lord Buddha, which I heard led to truth and wisdom. Then my magician-teacher also came to realise that he too had committed many black deeds. He began to fear the evil karma he had created and decided to learn more about the Holy Dharma for himself. He gave me customary parting gifts and allowed me to leave to find a true teacher for myself.

At first I found a holy teacher, a lama, who tried to teach me how to meditate. He said that fortunate people could achieve Buddhahood in a single day. In my arrogance I thought that since I had learned to cast spells in only fourteen days, surely I would be purified right away and become a Buddha. So instead of meditating, I spent my time sleeping! When the lama found out, he said he

could not help me, and told me to find Marpa the Translator. When I heard Marpa's name I remembered his reputation as a great teacher and, filled with unspeakable joy, I hurried to find him.

I arrived in this valley where I met a fierce-looking corpulent man — Marpa himself. He is both a great lama and a wealthy householder. I offered him my body, speech and mind and asked for food, clothing and teachings. I told him of all the suffering I had caused through my black magic. He said to me that I must choose either teachings or food and

38

clothing. I chose teachings. I must make do with what people give me for alms. Sometimes Marpa's wife, Dagmema, gives me food in secret. She is like a kind mother to me when my own poor mother is so far away.

But Master Marpa has not yet given me teachings. First he said that before he would teach me, I must bury two neighbouring valleys in hail because of the wicked people who lived there and preyed on pilgrims. He also told me to cast a spell on the bandits living in the nearby mountains. Using my magic, I did as he ordered. The hail frightened

the evil people into behaving better and my spell caused the bandits to fight among themselves. Despite my success, he still would not give me teachings. Now he says I must build him a special stone tower, but he keeps changing his mind about the shape and location of the tower. This is the fourth time I have begun one. The other times he angrily made me tear my work down and move it. He said he could not have told me to build them there or there, and in this shape or that. Perhaps this fourth tower will be right for him. I hope so because my back is getting very sore!

You might wonder why I am willing to obey all the strange commands of my lama. It's partly because if I die before I find true religion, with such evil deeds in my past, I'm certain to suffer in the realms of hell! But also, whenever I see Marpa, I am filled with love and respect for him, no matter how hot-tempered he is with me. I am certain that he knows what he is doing. And his wife Dagmema never fails to encourage me. I will just have to show him again and again that I am willing to do whatever he asks if only he will show me the true path to enlightenment.

Well, I must get back to work. Good fortune to you, wherever you are headed.

39

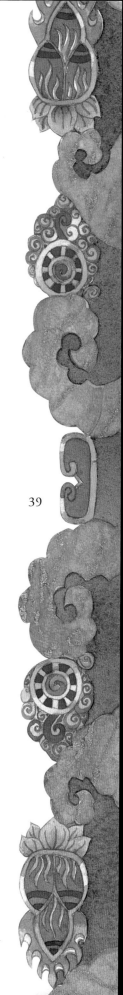

40

Milarepa finally received teachings from Marpa, after finishing the fourth tower. By then, his back was a mass of sores, but the boy had not given up. Marpa made him undergo other ordeals as well. When Marpa finally did accept Milarepa as a disciple, he revealed that all the trials he had put him through were ways of atoning for his evil deeds. Until he had been purified, Milarepa could not truly hear Marpa's teachings.

Milarepa studied with Marpa for several years. He was taught the Buddha's teachings of compassion and slowly learned how to stop clinging to confused ideas and performing misguided deeds. He also found out that Marpa had known all along that he would be one of his greatest students. Then the time came when Milarepa had to set out on his own.

First he went home to find that his mother had died and that his sister had wandered off as a beggar. Heartbroken, Milarepa vowed to leave the world until he had gained enlightenment. After making peace with his aunt and uncle, he spent many long, lonely years as a hermit in the high mountains of

Tibet. He wore only a cotton garment even in the coldest winters, ate nettles for food, grew thin as a skeleton and endured many hardships. He would never give up, though, and meditated without rest. Not until he had achieved the same state of peace and compassion taught by the Buddha did he return to civilisation.

Milarepa grew famous throughout Tibet. People flocked to him for teachings about the Buddhist path and he shared his understanding with everyone. Tibetans loved him because he was an ordinary person like themselves. It gave them hope that it was possible to have done stupid and cruel things, to feel remorse for those deeds, and to make amends.

They also loved him for his songs. Milarepa had a gift for putting his understanding into beautiful melodic poems, known as 'dohas'. All of them were full of the wisdom, joy and kindness he had found by following his lama's instructions. Collected together, they came to be called 'The Hundred Thousand Songs of Milarepa', and today they are treasured as one of the greatest works of literature in Tibetan history. Here is a small sample:

41

> *Like sun and moon in all their glory,*
> *Meditate clearly without darkness.*
> *Honour all beings as your dear parents,*
> *Love and show compassion to them.*

A thousand years after Milarepa, Tibetans still remember him as their great saint who was once a sinner. Since 1959, much of Tibetan culture has been destroyed by the Chinese Communists after they invaded and annexed Tibet. Believing that religion is poison, they killed Buddhist teachers and students and pulled down their monasteries and shrines. But one monument still stands: the final tower that Milarepa built. It is still a shrine for pilgrims who want to discover the kind of love and compassion in their hearts that can never be destroyed.

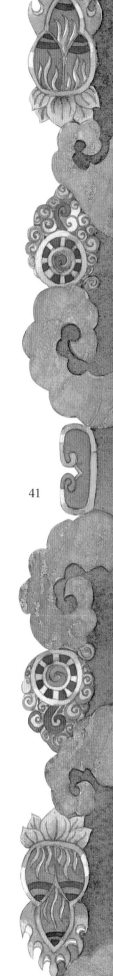

CAPTIVE PRINCESS

POCAHONTAS
North America

The year is 1613, and you have travelled to the early colonial times in what Europeans call the New World. You are on an English ship on a river in the tidelands around the Chesapeake Bay. The English have been trying to found a colony nearby, which they have named Virginia, centred around a fort called Jamestown. Right now they are pulling up anchor after a trading session with a village belonging to the Potomac tribe. However, you are not here to meet anyone English, but a native girl, a daughter of Powhatan, mighty chief of all the tribes for miles around here. She is not on board the ship by choice: she

has been kidnapped. Her name is Pocahontas. She is being kept locked in a cabin, but you bribe her jailer to let you in to talk with her. When you enter the cabin, she is looking out of the small porthole as the ship sails down the river past the village she had been visiting. Pocahontas is seventeen or eighteen years old, dressed in deerskin trimmed with shells and beads. Her hair is cut short in front and hangs longer at the back. Shells dangle from her pierced ears and you notice tattoos on her upper arms. Among the colonists, Pocahontas is famous for having saved one of their leaders, John Smith, and adopted him

as her brother. That was six years ago, when she was only eleven or twelve. She used to visit the colonists often after that, but she has not been seen in years, not since John Smith returned to England. Why would the colonists want to kidnap her now?

Pocahontas's beautiful dark eyes flash, her cheeks are flushed, yet she is not weeping or behaving as though she is afraid. When she sees you, she invites you in with head held high. You explain that you would like to help her if you can, and you ask if she knows why she has been kidnapped and where she is being taken to.

44

Thank you for your kindness, but I will come to no harm. Yes, I know what is happening. It breaks my heart. Sometimes I long for the old times, before I ever saw white men. I was almost twelve then, almost grown, and the favourite daughter of Powhatan, our chief who has united so many Algonquian tribes.

I miss those times now. Each day we children had our tasks: boys to learn to hunt and fish, to make weapons and build dugout canoes; girls to learn to tend the gardens, to make clothing, pottery and baskets. We also swam, told stories, sang and danced and played games of chase in the great deep forest. I was so happy and playful that I was called Pocahontas, the 'Frisky One'. On special mornings, like the beginning of the Spring plantings, our whole village would

meet at the river bank before dawn to greet the rising Sun, giver of light and warmth. As it rose, we would shout our joy and thankfulness and offer tobacco and sweet grass. Those were good times.

But an evil time followed. White-faced strangers on moving islands — ships like this one — began arriving. Sometimes they wanted to trade with our people, sometimes to kidnap or kill us. None of our warriors knew how to treat these men, who on one day would shoot murderous thunder out of sticks and on another day offer to trade copper kettles and beads for food. Some villages became friendly with them and others became enemies. But there was never trust between our people and theirs.

No white men had ever come to my father Powhatan's city, but of course, as a great chief he was disquieted by these intruders. He had not yet decided how to treat them, when one day his warriors brought him a prisoner, John Smith. I was sitting near my father when he was brought in, tied hand and foot. He had blue eyes like the sky and light hair growing out of his pink face, and he wore strange clothing, but I could see that he was not afraid, just as a good warrior of my tribe would not be. I liked him.

My father had him untied and we gave this John Smith a feast. He claimed to be a great chief, too. He showed us a round object with a whirling arrow inside it, which he called a compass. It always pointed to the north. All during the feast, some of my father's warriors demanded the white man's death. Others wanted us to treat him with kindness so that he would return to his people and tell them we were friends. My father and I never said a word to each other, but he looked at me in a special way during the feast. I knew what he wanted me to do.

So when he ordered his warriors to throw John Smith down and take up clubs to crush his head, I did what I had to do. In front of them all, I threw myself over him and stopped the execution. I claimed the ancient right of a woman to adopt a prisoner into our tribe. John Smith was now my brother and Powhatan's adopted son. From now on, the English people would be regarded as one of Powhatan's other tributary tribes, and we would trade with them: food and protection in return for metal tools and weapons. John Smith agreed and we returned him to his village called Jamestown. In this way we hoped to make peace between our peoples.

45

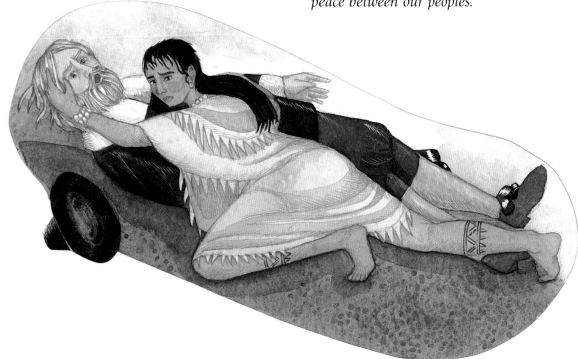

But John Smith did not give my father weapons, just more kettles and glass beads. These English still acted as though they did not trust us. So the peace did not last. Soon there were more kidnappings and killings, on both sides. I had to go to their Jamestown with gifts to get some of my people released. After that my father's messengers and I came to Jamestown often to visit my brother, John Smith, and our English people. I liked being friends with John Smith. He gave me gifts and taught me English words. I learned to say, 'Love you not me?' I would ask him that and then laugh.

I became friends with many of the people there. I played chase with the boys and learned to do what they call cartwheels. All the white people were grateful to me for saving John Smith's life, and for the gifts we brought our new friends. That winter they would have starved to death without our help. Yet still they did not respect us.

Once they visited my father and insisted on putting a crown on his head, saying the English king had sent it to him. They were trying to trick him into becoming a child of the English chief, as John Smith has become a child of our tribe. He did not want this: he is a great chief in his own right!

Another time, when the English came to our village to trade, fighting broke out. My father grew angry and wanted to kill my brother, John Smith, but I could not let that happen. I saved his life a second time by warning him and helping him

46

escape. Then my father decided we were no longer safe where we lived, and our whole village moved further away from the white men. The English then tried to force other villages to trade with them. Even my brother and friend John Smith behaved badly. Once he threatened my father's brother, chief of one of our villages, by holding a gun to his chest. No one behaved with honour.

John Smith disappeared one day. His people told us he was dead. My father was sorry to hear this, because though John Smith was a hard man, they had once understood and respected each other. Now there was even more trouble between the white people and my people. Over the past six years, more and more English have arrived to replace the first ones, who have mostly died of disease and starvation — and war with my people. It made me sad that we could not live in peace with each other. And I have always missed my brother, John Smith, and our happy times together. I no longer went to visit Jamestown any more. As a princess, I had other duties. My father saw that I was a good person to send to other tribes to collect tribute and to negotiate peace and trade agreements. I have been doing those things since then.

That is why I was in the village where I was captured. I was a guest of the village chief. His younger brother helped the English trick me on to their ship, and then he let the English seize me in exchange for a copper kettle! I know what the English want. They say that because I am Powhatan's favourite daughter, they can hold me for ransom, or force him to make peace with them. If being kidnapped would help bring peace between our two peoples, I would be glad to make that sacrifice. Will you tell the English this for me?

47

Did Pocahontas's hopes for peace come true? Yes, for a short time she was able to achieve peace between her people and the English settlers. It came about like this: after she was kidnapped, the colonists sent messengers to Powhatan, demanding he make peace, return his English prisoners, and surrender all the guns his people had obtained from the colonists over the years. But Powhatan was not willing to make peace on those terms, even for the sake of his daughter. Pocahontas spent a year in captivity.

During that year, she lived as a guest with a Christian minister who wanted to convert her to his faith and to teach her how to behave as an English lady. Pocahontas cooperated. Perhaps because of the minister's kindness, perhaps out of curiosity, or perhaps because of disappointment in her father, she became a Christian lady, baptised as Rebecca. She no longer did the things that had made her part of her tribe. Instead she now spoke English, wore English clothes, walked with small steps and modestly bowed head. She became a child of her new tribe, the English.

And she fell in love with an Englishman, John Rolfe. He asked for her hand in marriage and she accepted. Together they visited her father, Powhatan, to announce their decision. To everyone's surprise, Powhatan was delighted, and offered to make peace with the English. He was eighty years old now, and tired of war. For the next eight years, his people lived in relative harmony with the English. It was called the Peace of Pocahontas.

For a while Pocahontas/Rebecca helped her husband on his successful tobacco farm. Then she and a few other members of Powhatan's village sailed to England, hoping to show the English that her people were not savages. She and her husband arrived in Plymouth, England, in 1616 when she was twenty-one. By now she had a little son, Thomas. She became the talk of London as she visited everywhere in the huge city, always carrying herself as a princess. She even met the king and queen, dressed in proper English court costume, and introduced as Lady Rebecca. An artist painted her portrait to celebrate the occasion. But her health suffered in the damp, dirty city.

She also found out that John Smith was still alive and living in London. Pocahontas/Rebecca waited in vain for a visit from him. Only when she had been in England for months did he at last come to see her, appearing at her

door without warning. She was so overcome with emotion that she could not speak for several hours. When she was finally able to speak she reminded him of their old friendship and of all the kindness she had shown him and his people.

'They did tell us always you were dead,' she told him. She explained how she had grieved for her 'brother' all those years. She also said: 'You did promise Powhatan what was yours should be his, and the like to you; you called him Father, being in his land a stranger, and by the same reason so must I do you... I tell you I will, and I will be forever and ever your countryman.' John Smith was embarrassed by her insistence that she must call him 'Father' now, and that they were forever countrymen. As he took his leave she must have wondered, 'Love you not me?' Yet John Smith did still care about his young friend. He had even written to the queen requesting an audience for her. We will never know just why he took so long to make such an important visit.

Pocahontas fell ill and died before she could return home. John Rolfe returned to America without her, leaving their son in England. The Peace of Pocahontas ended when Powhatan's brother became great chief, the same man John Smith had once held at gunpoint. With every reason to hate the English, he engineered a horrible massacre of many colonists. John Rolfe, Pocahontas's husband, died around this time. No one knows if he was one of the victims.

But Pocahontas's son, Thomas, grew up in England. He returned to his mother's homeland when he was twenty, to discover that his grandfather, Powhatan, had left him thousands of acres of land. His many descendants still live in Virginia, proud that their ancestor was the girl who had tried to make peace between peoples so that each would become the countryman of the other.

COURAGEOUS COMPANIONS

ANNE SULLIVAN & HELEN KELLER
North America

50 You are going forward in time to the year 1895 to visit two friends, the world-famous Helen Keller and her teacher, Anne Sullivan. You are sitting with Anne in rocking chairs on the front porch of Helen's home in Tuscumbia, Alabama, in the Southern USA. It is a hot, sultry day full of the scent of flowers, and you are drinking lemonade together. Annie, as her friends call her, is a dark-haired, plump young woman, quite pretty and a bit flirty as she fans herself in the heat.

Helen joins you on the porch, and the way she walks, reaching for a familiar table or chair to guide her, tells you she is blind. She is also deaf. You notice that she is a pretty girl, with blue eyes and short curly light hair. She is about fifteen, and her face, the way it keeps changing expression, reminds you of sunlight shining through dancing leaves. She is interested in you right away and asks if she may touch your face so she knows what you look like. Her speech is hard to understand. She has not been taught how to use her lungs and vocal muscles properly because no one has worked out how to do this yet. Helen is a pioneer of deaf speech. You agree to let her explore your features and she lightly runs her hands over your whole face. She smiles her thanks and gives

you a little kiss on the cheek. Then she
sits down and takes Annie's hand. She
sits and waits patiently as her teacher
begins her story. You notice at once that
Annie does not have a Southern accent.

52

Hello, glad to meet you. You're surprised that I'm not from around here? I was born in the North, near Boston, in 1866. My parents were from Ireland and they came to America to escape the Great Famine. For twenty years, a blight killed almost all the potato crops, and the Irish people starved. Thousands died, and thousands left the country simply to stay alive.

But when my parents arrived in America, the Land of Plenty, they found the same grinding, desperate life they'd hoped to leave behind. They had no education and my father had no skills. Things got worse because soon they had a growing family to feed. I was the eldest. When I was three, I started to lose my eyesight due to an infection called trachoma. My eyelids swelled and got

hard bumps under them that scratched and hurt. The world dimmed into a grey blur, full of vague dark shapes.

That wasn't all that went wrong. My poor mother fell ill with tuberculosis, and my little brother Jimmie was born with a hip already swollen with it. Only my younger sister came out healthy. What with the hard times, my father turned to drink. When I was small, he had taken me on his knee and told me wonderful stories about Ireland, but we both changed. I turned into a little brat, and if he was drunk, he would fly into rages and beat me — if he could catch me!

When I was eight, my mother died. My father couldn't — or wouldn't — take care of us. Some of our relatives had also come over from Ireland, and they

had to take us in. My younger sister was easy to care for because she was healthy, but no one wanted my little brother and me — a boy with TB and a rude, almost blind little girl. I didn't help things with my fits, but no one seemed to see that I just needed someone to love me. It was so hard to be poor and blind, and to lose your parents and have your family broken up.

I suppose my relatives did their best, but they soon gave up on me and little Jimmie. One day when I was nine, a man came and took us away. We enjoyed the train ride he took us on, but then we had to ride to our new home in a horrid dark carriage for criminals called a Black Maria. 'Home' was the almshouse at Tewkesbury, Massachusetts, better known as the poorhouse. All the unwanted ended up there — the old, the simple, the sick and crippled, the crazy, the young women with babies and no husband…and us, the only two children in the whole place.

At first they tried to separate Jimmie and me, and put him in with the men. For once my temper was useful, and I 'persuaded' them to change their minds. He was all I had left. I tried to take care of him, but within two months my little brother died in the night. I wanted to die as well, I felt so alone.

The poorhouse was a nightmare that lasted nearly five years. Rats everywhere, bugs in the food, cold in the winter, and thin patched clothes to wear. But I made a few friends. One was a priest who arranged for a doctor to operate on my eyes, but the operations failed, and just left me feeling disappointed and bitter. Another friend was an old woman with such bad arthritis that she couldn't even sit up. But her eyes worked just fine. She would read to me as I turned the pages. She found out that my secret desire was to go to school, and she encouraged me. My aunt and uncle had said that school was a waste of time for a blind child, and I'd never had any education, just like my parents. But without schooling, what hope could I have in life?

One day I found out that some inspectors were coming to Tewkesbury Almshouse to see about reforming it, and I decided to ask them to let me go to school. After all, I was now fourteen, and couldn't even spell my own name! So, the day they arrived, I followed them everywhere, those great dark shapes, and tried to work up the courage to ask them. The men were actually at the gate, about to leave, when I threw myself into the middle of the group and begged to be allowed to go to school.

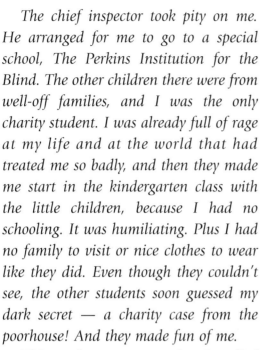

The chief inspector took pity on me. He arranged for me to go to a special school, The Perkins Institution for the Blind. The other children there were from well-off families, and I was the only charity student. I was already full of rage at my life and at the world that had treated me so badly, and then they made me start in the kindergarten class with the little children, because I had no schooling. It was humiliating. Plus I had no family to visit or nice clothes to wear like they did. Even though they couldn't see, the other students soon guessed my dark secret — a charity case from the poorhouse! And they made fun of me.

This made me so angry that I studied harder than anyone else. I would show them! I wasn't very nice to my teachers, either. They nicknamed me Miss Spitfire! I was always in trouble for being rude or disagreeing with them, but somehow we all survived, and several teachers took extra time to work with me. One or two even became my special friends. I'll always be thankful for their kindness.

And when I graduated, my classmates chose me to give the farewell speech at the ceremony. I shall never forget the beautiful white dress a friend of mine made for me, trimmed with lace and with a pink sash and a bouquet of pink roses at my waist. And…white shoes. I had never

had anything so beautiful to wear in all my life! I knew I looked lovely that day, even though I got such stage fright that I almost forgot my speech.

How did I know? Because, besides the joy of learning to read and write, of studying mathematics and science and history, another miracle happened while I was at Perkins. I was sent to a doctor who gave me back my sight. It took over a year and several operations, but when I graduated from Perkins, I could see! Not perfectly, and my eyes still hurt, but it is wonderful to see blue sky and bright sunshine, to know the face of a friend. And with glasses I can read regular books instead of Braille books, which are very tedious. Braille is a system of raised dots that stand for letters and numbers. You run your fingers over the dots to read.

But back to my story. They let me stay at Perkins after I regained my eyesight, because there was nowhere else for me to go. But, after graduating, I had no idea what to do. I was still too blind to do most kinds of work, and there are few jobs for women, anyway. But amazingly, I was offered a job as a teacher for a little seven-year-old blind girl. However, she was also deaf, and had been since she was a toddler. I was terrified, but I jumped at the chance, and that is how I came to meet my lovely Helen.

54

55

It hasn't been easy. Helen was a wild child when we first met. She knocked out two of my teeth shortly after I arrived. And I'm a fiery Yankee, living in the Deep South. It has not been that long since the Civil War, and bitterness lingers. We Yankees defeated those Southern slave owners, but many white people here still treat Negroes badly, and they hate people from the North. When I see the injustices around me, my blood boils.

Still, coming here was the start of my real life. Helen is its centre now, and so dear to me. She is destined for greatness. She has such a loving heart. Like when she was ten and heard about a three-year-old blind-deaf boy who was

so neglected that he still hadn't learned to sit up. She raised funds from rich people in Boston to help bring him to The Perkins Institution. We were living there ourselves then…but that's another story.

It's Helen's turn now. You heard her speak before with her own voice. She's only the second blind-deaf person in history to learn how to speak aloud, and it's been hard work. She's wanted to master speech since she was eleven, and she's proud of her success. But it's simpler if she spells her story into my hand using the finger alphabet. I'll interpret what she 'says'. But please — if you learn this way of communicating, don't let Helen know my sad tale. She's so full of innocence and love, she couldn't begin to understand.

*T*hank you for coming to hear my story. I was born here in Tuscumbia in 1880. My parents say I was eager to walk, talk and learn, but when I was nineteen months old, I fell ill with a high fever. I remember the pain and a hot white light. I nearly died. When the fever left me, my world had gone dark. Imagine a night with no stars or moon, no light at all, nothing to tell you where you are or what is around you. And I could hear nothing, not even my own breath. I was cut off from the world almost completely.

So I learned to use my sense of touch and smell and taste. I followed my mother around by hanging on to her skirts. She would hold me in her arms and I could feel her love for me and smell the fragrant roses on the table next to us.

But I lost all the words I had learned. As I grew older, I made up signs for things I wanted, like pretending to open an ice-box and shiver when I wanted ice cream. I nodded my head for 'yes' and shook it for 'no', just as you do.

But even though I could get around easily, I lived like a phantom in a no-world. And I got frustrated, not being able to see or talk or listen. I got so angry sometimes that I broke things and fought the very people who loved me. And they felt so sorry for me that they let me do all sorts of mischief. I didn't know better, and they didn't know how to reach me.

My uncle thought I was 'mentally defective' and said I should be put away in an institution for the mentally ill. My parents wouldn't listen to him, but one day when I locked my mother in the

pantry and kept the key hidden for hours, they knew something had to be done. They visited the famous scientist and teacher of the deaf, Alexander Graham Bell. Maybe you'll be lucky enough to meet him, too, one day. He recommended The Perkins Institution for the Blind, and they recommended Teacher. That's what I call her.

When she arrived, she was ready to love me. Somehow she understood all the rage that had built up inside me. She gave me a doll and made the word D-O-L-L into my hand with sign language. I copied her, but it meant nothing to me. And soon I was off on another round of destruction. So, before she could truly begin to teach me, she had to tame me. My parents had always let me have my own way in everything. At mealtimes I would wander around the dinner table grabbing food from other people's plates and messing it up. I've already told you about the tantrums I threw when I couldn't get what I wanted. When they weren't feeling sorry for me, they were afraid of me!

Teacher took me off to a nearby cottage on our property, and we lived alone together for a few weeks while she taught me basic manners. It was a hard and painful process, but we both won in the end. She taught me the right way to

behave, but she never tried to break my spirit. And once I had learned how to control my temper and wilfulness, she began to teach me words and letters. She would give me something to touch and then she would make signs into my hand. At first I was like a little monkey. I imitated everything she did, but I didn't quite understand what she was up to.

Then one day, about a month after she had arrived, she was getting me a cup of water from the pump. She gave me the cup and spelled C-U-P into my hand. Then she held my hand under the gushing water and spelled W-A-T-E-R into my hand. At that moment, an inner light dawned in me. Those signs were the names for what I was touching. That meant that everything had a name! I got so excited that I dropped my cup and fell to the ground to pat it. She gave me the name, G-R-O-U-N-D. She saw right away that I had finally understood what she was giving me: the gift of language. I was no longer cut off in my no-world.

Within days I had learned so many words that I started signing in my sleep. But I always wanted more, and she gave it to me. Teacher took me into the real world and restored it to me through touch and taste and smell. She put an egg into my hand and a baby chick pecked its way out. She caught a butterfly and let

57

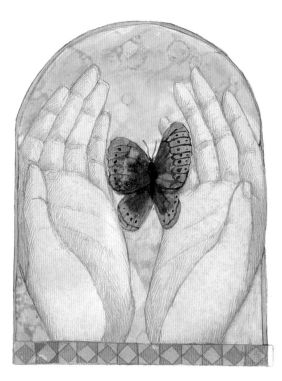

58

me cup it gently in my hands to feel its fluttering wings. She took me to the river bank and built a map of the world out of mud for me to feel. She taught me about flowers and birds and clouds and sunshine, about colours and feelings and...and everything she could. My hands have become my ears and eyes, and my other senses work with them to help me understand. Why, I can tell the difference between a white and a purple lilac just from their shape and scent. I can do the same with people, too.

I learned about ideas as well as things. I learned to name my emotions, to be able to say 'I love you' and know what it meant. When Teacher freed me, I lost most of my anger. I will always love her for what she did for me, and for what she keeps on doing. She's been everywhere with me, to meet famous people and to go to wonderful places like the Niagara Falls and the Chicago World's Fair. Everywhere I go, people are so kind and loving to me. They give me special permission to touch things so that I can 'see' them. And Teacher describes the world to me so wonderfully that I can imagine it for myself.

She's helped me get a good education as well, at the Perkins Institution and with other teachers. I've decided to go to college, you see. I wanted to go to Harvard, but that's only for men, so now I want to go to its sister school, Radcliffe. I need to prepare for the kind of work I want to do, helping normal people understand that people like me belong here in the world, too, not shut off from it in institutions, as though we're an embarrassing secret. Radcliffe is very difficult to get into, and it will mean hard work for Teacher and me, but I want to prove to the world that people like us, with handicaps, are just like you. We want to be part of the world, not shut off from it. Teacher's eyes are bad, too, so she understands me. Together I know we can do it!

With Annie's help, Helen did reach her goals, and more. Besides her other subjects, she learned French, German and Latin. After she was accepted into Radcliffe, Annie sat with her, spelling every lecture into her hand. She also read textbooks into Helen's hand. Then the girl had to remember it all. She graduated with honours, a first for a blind-deaf person.

Helen became a renowned author and lecturer. Working for the American Foundation for the Blind, she travelled around the world to campaign for the blind, and received a star's welcome. Promoting the cause of the blind and deaf, she helped thousands of people who might otherwise have endured 'no-worlds' like hers. During both World Wars she visited wounded soldiers to help them begin life again. Her religious faith led her to speak out for the rights of women and of people of colour, and to become a socialist and pacifist. Harvard University's first-ever honorary degree to a woman went to her.

She had fun, too. She learned to swim, to ride a bike, ride horses, even to dance. She starred in two movies about her life, and one won an Academy Award. She also met European kings and queens, several US presidents, and movie stars like Charlie Chaplin. Helen became one of the most famous and beloved women of her day.

And beside her was Annie Sullivan. In saving Helen from her dark lonely world, she had achieved what only a few people had ever done before, and many people acclaimed her as an educator of genius. They wanted to know her theories on education, and she gladly gave them: see what your students need, let them experience things for themselves, teach them through what interests them, and then what you want them to learn will come easily.

Annie remained a bit of a 'spitfire', always ready to protect Helen's welfare. Helen was grown up before Annie could bear to tell her about her own painful childhood. Helen was holding Teacher's hand when Annie died in 1936, totally blind, her eyes worn out with helping Helen to 'see'. Helen lived until 1968, still working for the deaf and blind, and always ready to greet a new friend with a kiss on the cheek.

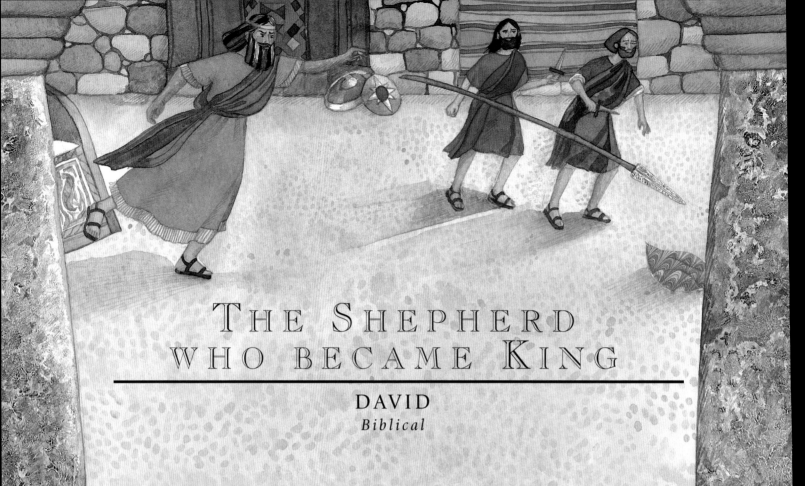

The Shepherd
who became King

DAVID
Biblical

You are leaping back in time now, to about 1000 BC. You're in the city of Gibeah, sitting in the throne room of King Saul, first King of Israel. The room is constructed from rough-cut stones and decorated simply. Light from the setting sun streams through the small windows and you feel a warm breeze flow past you, carrying the scent of almond and olive trees into the room. Around you, several men, soldiers by the look of them, sit cross-legged or stand by the wall. They all wear short tunics under colourful mantles which are thrown over their shoulders and belted to their waists. A few carry short

knives bound to their left arms. King Saul, a grim-faced, bearded older man, sits on a carved stone throne, his head thrown back and his eyes closed. His mantle is royal purple and he wears a simple crown, but otherwise he is dressed like the men around him. A javelin leans on the throne by his side.

A slender, handsome youth of perhaps eighteen is singing while he plays a harp-like instrument called a kinnor. His name is David. He has curly dark hair, bright eyes and red cheeks, and an enchanting voice. He is singing a victory song, but rather than merely listing brave deeds, this song is also a prayer of

thanks to the Hebrew God. The words tell you that the Philistines, the Israelites' worst enemy, have been defeated in a great battle. The song should make the king glad, since it mentions his brave leadership, but as Saul listens, his face contorts into a hideous snarl. He opens his eyes, grabs the javelin and hurls it at David. The youth ducks just in time. Everyone scrambles to their feet and, in the confusion, David slips out of the door and runs down the steps. You follow close behind him.

You catch up with him as he flees and ask him what is going on. He stops to catch his breath, and you see that instead of fear there is sorrow written on his face. As you both walk through the deepening night out of the large royal courtyard and into the narrow streets of the city, he tells you his story.

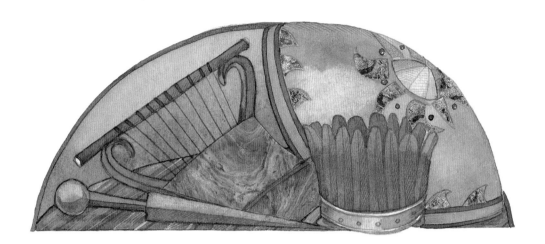

62

*A*las Yahweh, our Lord God, has been sending my king a black spirit over the last few years, ever since the great prophet Samuel cursed him for disobeying the Lord. What did Saul do? It happened before a great battle. Samuel was to perform a sacrifice, and he was late. Fearing that his men would desert him before Samuel arrived, Saul performed the sacrifice instead. The prophet Samuel was furious. He warned Saul that by trusting in human strength and not in God's, God had withdrawn his blessings from him and his heirs. Saul had lost the right to the throne of Israel. Now the king lives in constant fear and distrust, not knowing when or how the Lord will punish him.

When I was younger, I had the power to soothe my king's black spirit with my songs. He had heard of my singing and sent for me. I was a mere shepherd boy then, but someone had told him of my musical ability. For two years, I stayed at his side as his minstrel and personal attendant.

But war broke out again, and Saul sent me back to my father's house, where I returned to my duties as a shepherd. I was sorry to go. I wanted to join my brothers in fighting, but with them gone, my father needed me at home to guard the flocks day and night. Being a shepherd can be as dangerous as being a soldier. Once a lion tried to steal one of the lambs and, another time a bear attacked the flock. I killed them both with my slingshot and knife!

But I still missed fighting in real battles, so I rejoiced when my father sent

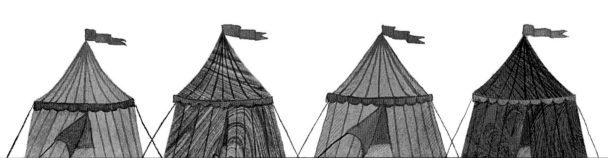

me to King Saul's camp with supplies for my brothers. At last I could see the war. When I arrived at the camp, I saw our army spread out on one side of the valley of Elah, and our enemy the Philistines on the other side, but clearly no fighting had occurred. Instead, the soldiers were all sitting by their tents, uneasy and ashamed. I asked my brothers what was going on. They told me that everyone was afraid because of a giant of a man named Goliath, the champion of the Philistines.

For the past forty days, Goliath had come to the edge of the river that divided the two armies and challenged us: if our champion could defeat him in single combat, then the Philistines would become our slaves. But if he won, then the tribes of Israel would become the slaves of the Philistines. When no one would accept the challenge, he mocked our nation and our God, and strutted back to his camp. King Saul had even offered a great reward for the man who defeated Goliath, including marriage to his daughter. I couldn't understand why no one would fight this Philistine windbag — until I saw him myself. Then I knew that our soldiers had reason to fear him. We Hebrews are not a tall people, but he was huge! Almost twice my height!

By then I had asked too many questions and someone thought I was volunteering to fight Goliath myself. When King Saul heard, he had me brought to him. Well, I did want to fight! After all, Goliath had insulted not only our nation but our faith. Saul tried to talk me out of this hopeless battle, since I was a shepherd, not a soldier, but I wanted to uphold my nation's honour. He even tried to lend me his own armour, but it was too big for me, and besides, I wasn't used to wearing it. Nor would it have been any use against a giant like Goliath. I thanked him but refused. The only true armour is the protection of our Lord.

So I crossed the shallow river, still hidden from the Philistines by the tamarisk trees that grew there. Deciding on my strategy, I picked up five perfect throwing stones from the river bed and put them in my pouch. What was good enough for a wild beast would be good enough for this pillar of a man.

When Goliath saw me, he laughed. All the while I was approaching him, he mocked my size and strength in his great booming voice, and I let him. He could have used his sword or spear against me, though I knew that my slingshot could shoot faster than he could run and further than he could throw. But he was so sure

63

of victory that he wanted to wait for me to reach him so he could kill me with his bare hands. His arrogance was his undoing. I called to him that my God was the only true protector, that his bones would soon be scattered on the plains. At the last moment, when I had got within just a few feet of him, I reached into my pouch, grabbed a stone and, within the blink of an eye, whirled my slingshot about my head and released the stone. It had to hit its mark just right, and the target was small: right between Goliath's eyes, where his helmet gave no protection.

For that instant, time seemed to slow down. I remember the flight of the little stone as it raced through the air, seeing the surprise on Goliath's face as it hit him, and watching him slowly topple over, like a huge ugly tree. The stone hit with such force that it knocked him down. While he lay there stunned, I rushed up, pulled his enormous sword from its scabbard and beheaded him.

It was the signal for the Israelite army to swarm against their enemy. The Philistines were caught unawares, not even armed because they had been so confident of victory. The soldiers of Israel overwhelmed them and the day was ours.

After the battle, Saul hailed me as the hero of the day. He welcomed me by his side and promised me great rewards.

He made me a leader in the army and we pursued further victories against the Philistines. I loved the army, and the men serving under me became my loyal followers. I became best friends with Saul's son Jonathan, and almost felt I was part of the king's family.

But months later, when we returned to our capital city of Gibeah, Saul's mood changed. People came out of the city to greet us, singing and dancing for joy. But what they sang was:

Saul has killed his thousands and David has killed his tens of thousands.

64

They meant it as praise for my battle with Goliath or perhaps as a sting to King Saul, who could have faced Goliath himself. Whatever they meant, the words poisoned my king's mind against me. He seems to fear that I covet his throne. My friend Jonathan has had to defend my loyalty to his father. When his dark spirit leaves him, my father-in-law regrets the harsh thoughts he has harboured against me.

Yes, I am now married, but instead of giving his eldest daughter to me as he had promised, Saul gave her to someone else. But his second daughter, Michal, is the one I was always drawn to, even when we were both very young. I was shy of becoming his son-in-law, as I am not wealthy. But having hinted that I should ask to marry Michal, Saul then told me that I must pay a bride price for her: proof that I had killed a hundred Philistines. So I did that, and more. I led my men on raids and killed two hundred of our enemies!

Now Michal and I are married. We love each other dearly, but even our love seems to make King Saul jealous. That and the victories I have continued to achieve over the Philistines. Perhaps that is why he threw the spear at me tonight. I have tried to stay by his side in the hope that he will recover. But lately even my music fails to soothe him. I do wonder, though, if someone has told him of the time the prophet Samuel came to my father's house. It wasn't long after he had given his fatal warning to King Saul. He inspected all my brothers and then called for me — I was out tending the sheep as usual. When he saw me, he said, 'This is the one,' and anointed my head with scented holy oil. None of us knew what it meant. Now that I am married to Michal, perhaps it means that I am to succeed Saul. But that is all in the hands of the Lord. I would no more reach for the throne than harm Jonathan. King Saul wants him as his heir, and I wish for that, too.

We've reached the house that the King gave to Michal and me — although it may not be safe to stay here much longer. Thank you for walking back with me. Good night.

65

That night, Saul sent men to wait outside David's home and kill him when he came out the next morning. Michal, alert to her husband's danger, insisted that he flee the city. She helped him escape out of the window and then made up their bed in a way that looked as though David was sleeping in it. When the assassins bullied their way into the house the next morning, they were fooled into thinking David was ill and still sleeping. Only when Saul demanded they bring David to him, bed and all, was the ruse discovered. When Saul questioned Michal, she pretended that David had threatened her and made her help him.

66

She was not to see her husband again for years, and during that time her father married her to another man.

David tried to return to Saul, hoping that the madness had passed, but Saul was beyond reason by then. Warned by his dear friend Jonathan, David fled with a few followers into exile. He became an outlaw for many years, and even lived with the Philistines for a while. Twice he had the opportunity to kill Saul when the king was alone or sleeping. But out of respect for kingship and the desire to let things unfold according to his God's wishes, not his own, David held back.

Finally, not only Saul but Jonathan was killed in yet another battle with the Philistines. David, mourning for his lost friend and his mad father-in-law, came out of hiding to find that the people of the southern half of Israel, Judah, wanted him for their new king. Having accepted their acclamation, he ruled there for seven years, much of his time spent in battle with enemies. He was reunited with Michal, although over the years their love for each other had dimmed.

At last, after a painful civil war, both the northern and southern tribes of Israel became united under King David's leadership, and he ruled all Israel for thirty more years. He had come a long way from his days as a shepherd boy.

In those years David became the ideal Israelite king. He continued to put his trust in his Lord first, and all his actions sprang from that fountain of faith. He was just, brave, loving and firm. All the other kings who followed had to measure up to the standard he set. He also continued to compose new prayers of praise to his God. Many of these have been preserved in the Book of Psalms in the Hebrew and Christian holy scriptures. People still turn to his psalms for strength in difficult times, particularly the twenty-third psalm, which begins, 'The Lord is my Shepherd'. And when Christianity became a separate religion from Judaism, it was of key importance that Jesus of Nazareth belonged to the line of King David.

David has continued to be a much-loved figure to the present day. Sculptors and painters throughout the ages have been inspired to create images of him, while children still thrill to the story of his brave stand against Goliath. That story has come to be a symbol of how those who are small and weak can resist the oppression of the huge and mighty, not by strength but by faith.

THE TENNESSEE TORNADO

WILMA RUDOLPH
North America

68   Let us visit another girl from the Southern USA. It is a hot sticky morning in Clarksville, a small town about fifty miles from Nashville, Tennessee. The year is 1949, and you are in a school yard in a poor black neighbourhood, looking for a girl named Wilma Rudolph. The playground is full of children running, jumping and playing. When you ask after Wilma, it seems as though half of the children you meet are her brothers or sisters. They lead you towards a pretty nine-year-old sitting by herself watching a basketball game. She's watching so closely that at first she does not notice you and you wonder why she does not join in the game herself. Then you see the brace on her leg. The basketball suddenly bounces out of the court and she almost catches it as it flies over her head, but it is just out of reach. One of the players runs after it and starts to call her names and mock her for missing, then sees her older brothers and sisters. The child stops in mid-sentence and runs back to the game, looking ashamed. Clearly no one is allowed to make fun of Wilma when her family are around!

Wilma limps forward and introduces herself in a soft Southern drawl. You do not think you have ever seen such a skinny child. Her hair is tightly braided

and she is wearing a dress made out of a flour sack, as are the other Rudolph girls. The fabric of their dresses is a sure sign of poverty, but their clothes are all sewn with care. Wilma's eyes are so huge they seem to fill her thin face, but her smile is pure sunshine.

70

Hello. Let's sit down over here in the shade. It's mighty hot, isn't it? This heavy old metal brace and the ugly old shoe that goes with it get pretty hot, too. Why do I have to wear them? Because I had polio, when I was four years old. That was five years ago, in 1944. I've had that and scarlet fever and double pneumonia, not to mention all the regular childhood diseases like measles and mumps and chicken pox. Except I usually caught several things at the same time. I was born two months early, you see, and that made me weak. I weighed only four and a half pounds when I was born. Nobody knew if I'd live, because babies that small often die. My whole family worried about me. Maybe all the love and attention I got from my family is what gave me the strength to live. I have lots of brothers and sisters. Some of them died before I was born. If all of them had lived, there would have been twenty-two of us.

Anyway, I was always a sickly little thing. If one of my brothers or sisters became sick, I'd catch what they'd got, and then that sickness would just hang on for ever! But the worst was the polio. Most children die from it or are crippled for life. Some day maybe there'll be a vaccine for it. Yet Momma wouldn't give up on me. We're so poor, we can't really afford the one doctor in Clarksville who'll treat black people, but she decided I was going to get better, no matter what.

Twice a week, when she wasn't doing some rich white lady's laundry or house-keeping or sewing, she started taking me fifty miles on the bus to Nashville to the all-black medical college. We still go. They give me all sorts of massage treatments and baths and make me do special exercises. Now she and some of my brothers and sisters help me with those same exercises at home. They hurt like fire, but they work! I'm getting stronger.

I sure do like going on those bus rides, but there's one thing about them that seems wrong. All us black people have to ride at the back of the bus where it's stinky and hot. And if a white person wants to sit down, a black person has to give up her seat, even if she's some poor old grandma with sore feet. That's not

right, no way. I'd like to see that change some day — that and a whole lot of other rules about what black people can and can't do. I don't like being treated like I'm worthless because I'm black. Too many white folks think black people are 'shiftless and lazy'. They ought to meet my family! We know our worth. Momma and Daddy love us all, they work hard, and they would never go on welfare, no matter how poor we are. They're too proud, and I'm proud of them!

I'm going to surprise everyone and walk some day. Then Momma and I will send that old brace back to the college with a thank-you note that says: 'We don't need this any more. Our Wilma can walk!' But I'm not stopping there, no sir!

See all those children running around? Look over there where they're playing basketball. I watch them all the time, look to see what works and what doesn't — strategy, you know. I even make my older brothers let me play with them at home. I may move slowly, but I'm smart! We use a peach basket for a hoop, stuck up on a pole. I even play when they're not around. One of these days, I'm going to be out there with the rest of the kids, and I plan on being really good at basketball, and at running, and any other sport I choose. You just wait and see.

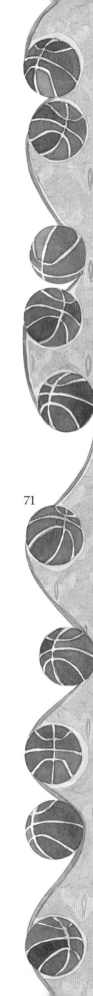

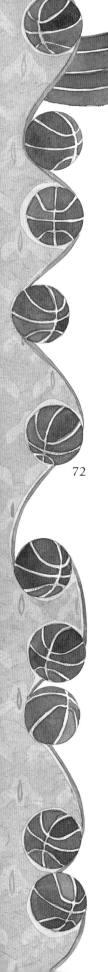

You will be glad to know that Wilma realised her dream, and much more. She did indeed get strong enough never to need a brace again. When she was ten, her mother went outside the house one day, and there was Wilma playing basketball all alone — without the brace! She'd been practising in secret, to surprise everybody. Wilma became a basketball star at secondary school, too. But that was only the beginning.

A famous college track coach named Ed Temple saw her at a basketball game and was so impressed that he began training her as a runner before she had even completed secondary school. Under his guidance, she became a champion track star. She ran her first Olympic race in Australia in 1956 when she was still at school, coming home with a bronze medal for her part in the relay race. By then she had grown to be six feet tall, but she was still skinny. She weighed only 89 pounds (40 kilograms).

Her talent and good grades won Wilma a sports scholarship to Tennessee State University, where Ed Temple taught. She was the first member of her family to go to college. While she was there, she joined the university's world-class track team, the Tigerbelles. With her team, she returned to the Olympics in 1960, in Italy.

By then, Wilma had already broken several world records for speed. But the Olympics were the big test. That year, they were to be on television for the first time and millions of people would be watching. Everyone had expected great things of her — until she twisted her ankle just days before the races were to begin.

In spite of her injury, Wilma won two gold medals in individual races. She also ran with her relay team, where she almost dropped the baton as her team-mate passed it to her. That mistake cost them precious time, and Wilma lagged behind for the last round. But in the last moments of the race, she burst from behind to win the race, and a third gold medal! She was the first American woman to win three gold medals at the Olympics, and shot to instant fame as the fastest woman in the world.

Wilma became a media star overnight. In Italy the newspapers hailed her as the 'Black Gazelle', in France they called her the 'Black Pearl', and in the US

72

she became the 'Tennessee Tornado'. Black people around the world took pride in Wilma's achievement. She met famous people like the Pope in Italy and President John Kennedy back home. She must have been especially proud to return to Clarksville, to a victory parade and banquet held in her honour: the first integrated event in the city's history.

By the age of twenty, Wilma had achieved all her goals as an athlete. She continued to win races, but despite the honours heaped on her at home and abroad, she decided to retire from sports in 1963. She had other aims in life now. One was to work to achieve stronger civil rights for black people. She joined the growing civil rights movement of the 1960s, using her fame to challenge the laws that segregated black and white people in schools, parks, buses, restaurants, hotels and the workplace.

Although Wilma married and raised a family, she never forgot another of her goals: to help other black youngsters. At that time, sports heroes did not make the kind of money they do today. No large companies were asking them to sponsor running shoes or other products. Sports men and women had to make ordinary livings just like everyone else. So Wilma chose work that meant something special to her. She dedicated her life to encouraging children, just as her family had once encouraged her.

She spent several years after college graduation as a teacher and coach, then worked for the US government helping to bring sports education programmes to children in inner-city ghettos. But she wanted to do more. She founded two organisations, Wilma Unlimited and the Wilma Rudolph Foundation, that allowed her to achieve all her different aims. Now she could coach, teach, lecture and provide scholarships for young people all over the US, to make their dreams come true, just as hers had. She also wrote an autobiography that was later made into a film. Wilma knew that if she could succeed despite the hardships she had faced, so could others. Although she died of cancer in 1995, the hope she brought to so many children will never die.

73

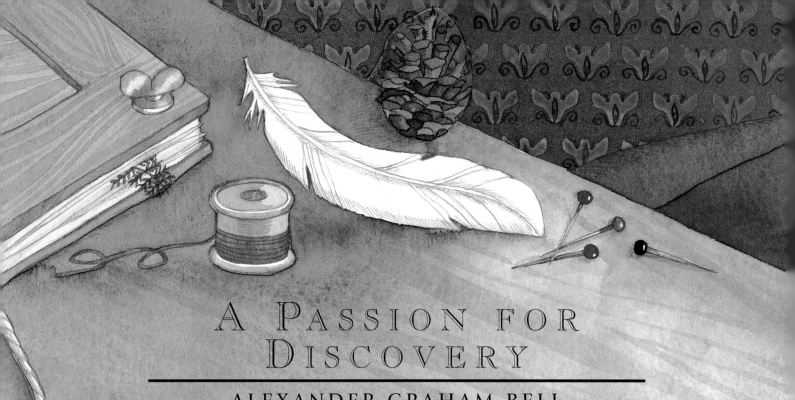

A Passion for Discovery

ALEXANDER GRAHAM BELL
Scotland

Now you have travelled almost ninety years back in time, to 1863. You are in the misty, cool city of Edinburgh, inside a fine house, and you are walking upstairs into what might once have been a children's nursery. A bright fire burns in the fireplace, although the room is much chillier than you would like. And what a clutter! Scattered on shelves and tables, littering the floor, everywhere you look your eye lights on something odd and interesting. There are dried plants, all labelled, and birds' eggs; animals, some stuffed and some pickled in jars; strange pieces of hand-made equipment; and bits of wood and cottonwool and nails and...too much to take in all at once.

Two boys, one about eighteen and the other about sixteen, are standing together at a workbench, tinkering with something. They turn as they hear you enter the room, and wave a greeting. The younger boy is the one you have come to visit. His name is Alexander Graham Bell; the other boy working with him is his elder brother, Melville, now whooping with excitement.

They call eager greetings to you, and you walk over to see what they are making. They have just finished. Before them on the workbench lies a crude

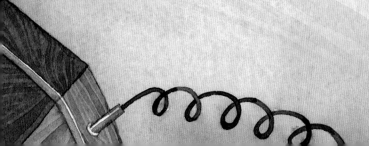

model of the speaking parts of a head: nose, cheeks, mouth, lips, tongue, larynx, and even teeth. Melville turns a crank as Alexander pushes and pulls levers, and the mouth opens and closes — and speaks the word 'Ma-ma'. The two boys invented the device themselves, for a bet with their father. Melville now excuses himself: he wants to fetch their father to show off their new contraption to him. While he's gone, Alexander explains what they have been doing.

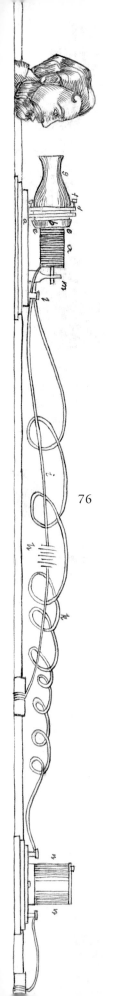

*C*all me Aleck. That way you won't confuse me with Father or Grandfather. They're named Alexander, too.

And what is this funny talking head about? Our father challenged Melville and me to build one after we saw a talking machine at the home of a professor friend of his. We are all very interested in speech in one way or another, you might say. After all, my grandfather teaches elocution and my father works with people who have problems like stuttering, and they are both famous for what they do. My father is fascinated by speech. He has written several books on its principles and, for years now, he has also been creating a system of written symbols that will describe any sound made by the human voice. For instance, it can be used to

describe the speech of an Irishman, brogue and all, or of an American, or a man from India, or an African Zulu, or even the way a sneeze sounds. All from the same symbols — a sort of universal alphabet of sounds. He calls his system Visible Speech.

I am interested in speech, and in hearing problems as well. After all, my mother is almost completely deaf. She's quite talented as an artist and as a pianist, although she has to use a hearing tube to listen to the notes. I'm the only person she can actually hear. I put my lips just by her forehead and speak in a deep voice so that she can make out the words. Otherwise, we have to use sign language. That means that a deaf person is limited to conversing with only those who know signs. Too many deaf people feel shut off

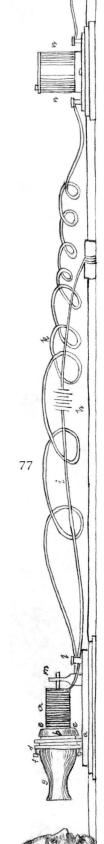

from the rest of the world, and they lead silent, lonely lives. Wouldn't it be wonderful if deaf people could speak as well, and then read lips, so they could be wholly part of the world you and I take for granted? That's something I would like to see happen, seeing how well my own mother manages. Hmm...I wonder if Visible Speech would work for teaching deaf people to speak?

But speech is only one of my interests. We live in a great age, the 'Machine Age', and every day someone invents something wonderful and new. I've been inventing things myself since I was ten or so. I figured out a way to husk wheat for a mill owner who lives near here. His son and I were getting into mischief at the mill one day, and the owner told us to do something useful instead. When I asked him how we might help, he gave me a handful of grain and said, 'Try to find a way to husk this.' And I did. Now he is using some equipment he already owned which I adapted so that it could rub off the wheat husks mechanically!

I've been fascinated by the world around me ever since I can remember. My earliest memory is sitting in the middle of a wheat field and trying to hear it growing. So I suppose that, for a long time, hearing has been as important to me as speaking. Perhaps that's why I also like to be on my own quite a bit, to wander through the countryside and lie in the sun-drenched Scottish heather. I like to listen to the world, to think and to dream, and to experiment.

I have lots of dreams and ideas. Sometimes they get in the way of what I'm supposed to be doing. I never did well at school, because I saw no point in repeating something I had already understood. Drill work just made me lose interest. My parents were disappointed in me, though. Like many children, my brothers and I had learned at home from Mother until we were ten. We loved learning from her. I collected birds' eggs and learned to identify plants, and to play the piano, and lots more besides.

And Father taught us, too. For instance, photography is still new and odd to most people, but not to us. Through my father, my brothers and I learned how to develop our own photographs. With such a promising beginning, my parents naturally expected me to do well at school. I wish I could have pleased them, but I became bored.

Finally, when I was fourteen, they despaired of me enough that I was sent to stay in London with my grandfather for a year. He turned me into a proper gentleman, though at first I hated all the dressing up and behaving with good

78

Now, though, I am back home. I will start to work as a teacher myself soon, at a private school on the north coast of Scotland. (Some of the students will be older than me!) I took the job because I want to be on my own.

My parents still think I'm a child, but I'm already sixteen and ready to see the world. In fact, had I not taken this teaching position, I might have run away to sea. I thought better of that, though.

I have the curious feeling that there's something special I must do in life, some purpose I need to fulfil. I suppose it sounds silly, but I want to really do something with my life, to make a difference...

Oh, here comes Melville with our father. I hope he likes our talking head!

manners. But Grandfather also became a companion and a friend. He taught me that our worth as human beings has nothing to do with wealth or social class because, with education, anyone can make something good of himself. He says education is like a ladder for climbing out of the depths of ignorance and misunderstanding. He inspired me to do something with my life, perhaps to teach. And of course, being a great elocutionist, Grandfather taught me that speech — sharing through communicating is what I think he means — is the greatest gift we humans have been blessed with.

Though he often irritated Aleck with sarcastic remarks and demands that he do better, Dr Bell also helped his son get started on his remarkable career. It began when tragedy struck. First the youngest Bell son, Ted, and then the eldest, Melville, fell ill and died of tuberculosis. In those days, tuberculosis was a dreaded killer, and no one knew how to cure it. The only treatment that had any effect was for the patient to move to a warmer, drier climate.

When Aleck, now in his early twenties, began to show signs of getting sick, his parents moved with him to a town in southern Ontario, Canada. There he continued to learn, to dream and to experiment. He became friendly with members of a Mohawk tribe living nearby, and used Visible Speech to record their language. The members of the tribe were so impressed that they made him an honorary member.

When his father's work teaching Visible Speech and working with deaf people grew too demanding, young AGB, as people called him, moved to Boston to take up part of the workload. For the rest of his life, Aleck split his home between Canada and the United States. He taught deaf children in Boston, and at the same time began his remarkable career as an inventor. There he also married one of his students, a beautiful, rich — and deaf — young lady. Her father backed Aleck while he was working on his early inventions, among them the one that made him not only wealthy but world-famous: the telephone.

From some reading he was doing on experiments in sending sound waves, Aleck had got the idea that someone had already sent speech along electrical wires. This was not in fact the case, but as a result of this misunderstanding, Aleck developed ideas that led him step by step to inventing the telephone. Of course, others were experimenting, too. Aleck obtained a patent for his invention only a few hours before a rival tried to patent a similar device.

Other inventions followed. From figuring out how to air condition his house to inventing flat discs for recording sound, Aleck was always busy. He also found time to work on the *National Geographic Magazine*, which his father-in-law had founded. When he started putting pictures and photographs in it, what had been a dull little science journal turned into a hit, first in the USA, then worldwide.

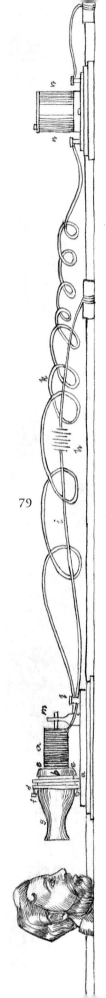

79

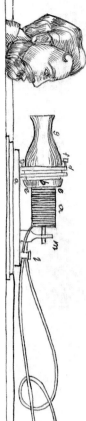

80

In later years, Aleck and his family bought property on Cape Breton Island in Nova Scotia, Canada. Its cool summers reminded him of the Scottish Highlands. There he built a huge summer home and continued his pursuit of any idea that caught his fancy, from trying to breed sheep that produced more than one lamb at a time to figuring out a way to obtain fresh water from salt water. One of his favourite projects was flight: from constructing kites to aeroplanes.

His was the first plane to fly in the British Empire, launched in Nova Scotia, near his summer home. He made flying safer, too, by inventing ailerons — wing flaps that move to keep the plane level. These are just a few of the experiments and inventions that flowed from Aleck's fertile mind. Some, especially the telephone, have changed the world for ever, by making communication easy, anywhere and at any time. And many of the modern developments of the telephone, like the use of fibre optics, stem straight from ideas Aleck worked on himself.

81

But none of these inventions were what Aleck felt most proud of. His greatest dream was to bring deaf people into the circle of ordinary life, not to see them set aside as second-class citizens. He worked for years to improve schooling conditions for deaf children, helped set up schools for the deaf, and continued teaching deaf children himself. He was also responsible for introducing Helen Keller, to her teacher, Anne Sullivan. He and Helen became lifelong friends, and, as we have seen, Helen in turn became famous for her own achievements.

By the time 'AGB' died, aged seventy-five, he had changed the world for ever, and for the good. Instead of conquering people, he built bridges of communication. The next time you call a friend, surf the Net, hear a CD or fly in an aeroplane, remember the boy who listened to the world and gave it a voice.

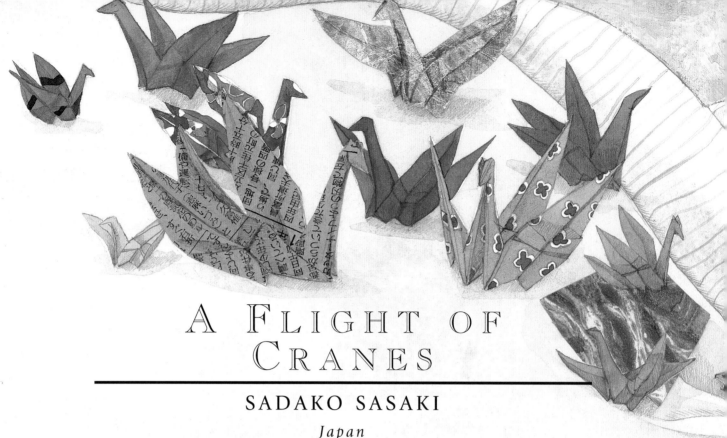

A Flight of Cranes

SADAKO SASAKI

Japan

Your next stop takes you to Hiroshima in Japan. It is the autumn of 1955 and you are walking through a hospital ward, being guided by a kindly nurse down a quiet corridor lined with doors. Behind each door is a room, and inside each room lies someone who is ill. Now and then another nurse or doctor glides by, on the way to see patients. You notice the faint hospital smell.

Your guide opens one of the doors for you, and instead of the dim, unwelcoming hospital room you expect to enter, you find a space filled with dancing colours. Everywhere you look, hundreds of strings of bright paper birds hang from the ceiling. There are long rows of tiny fluttering paper cranes. There are large individual cranes, shiny metallic cranes, many-patterned cranes, and dull newsprint cranes. Stirred by the breeze of the opening door, they look as if they could all surge right out of the hospital and into the sky.

You look around past the dazzling flock of paper birds and see a wheel-chair near the window, a small chest for clothing (a little wooden doll and a golden paper crane sit on top of it) and a hospital bed. Propped up in the bed is a pale twelve-year-old girl, almost as thin as a skeleton. She is trying to fold

a square of brilliant red paper into
the shape of a crane, but her fingers
fumble and her arms almost shake with
the effort. She drops her work with a
sigh of despair and then sees you. When
the nurse introduces you, the girl is too
weak to return your bow of greeting,
though she tries to smile. Her name is
Sadako Sasaki, and she is dying of a
form of cancer that affects the blood-
stream. It is called leukaemia.

The nurse tells you that you cannot
stay long, and softly closes the door. You
offer Sadako a little gift: some squares of
bright paper for making more cranes.

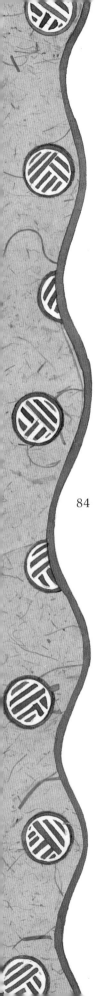

84

*T*hank you. You are very kind. I wish I could work faster, making cranes, but I am so tired these days that it's getting too hard to fold them. The art of origami — paper folding — is ancient. By folding paper, you can make all sorts of shapes, like frogs and dragons and birds. The crane is sacred in my home-land, and it carries our wishes to the heavenly realms of the gods.

I am working on my second set of a thousand cranes, hoping my wish will come true. There is a tradition in Japan that if a sick person folds a thousand cranes and wishes to get well, the gods will grant the wish. My mother made one for me and my roommate Kiyo when we were put in this room, and then some high school girls sent strands of cranes to those of us suffering from A-bomb disease.

I received one and Kiyo didn't. But that's when we decided to make a thousand cranes together, so our wish to get better might come true. Kiyo's wish is coming true, but mine has not, so I am trying again. I've lived longer than anyone expected me to, so maybe this time...

Since I came here my family and friends have been so caring. They visit and bring me special food, but I don't much feel like eating any more. Some of my classmates exchange letters with me — or they did. I tire so easily now, it's hard to write. They sent me this kokeshi doll, too, and paper for making more cranes. I use any kind: scraps from my father's barbershop, foil sweet wrappers, even labels off medicine bottles! I folded over six hundred so far, and for a while I did get better. But now, I don't know...

I used to be a champion runner. My mother said I could run before I could walk. I helped my class win the relay race on Field Day, and wanted to join the school team when I began at middle school. That would have been last spring. Only I never got to middle school — by then I was already in hospital. My illness started over a year ago, but I didn't know what was happening. I had dizzy spells, but I was sure I'd get over them, so I kept them a secret. Then one day I blacked out and my family took me here for tests. I never really left the hospital after that, except for short visits home.

I am very sick with leukaemia, the atom bomb disease. My gums are swollen and sore, my bones hurt, and I get terrible headaches, because I was exposed to radiation poisoning as a toddler. Our whole city was poisoned.

I remember what happened, even though I was so young. It was on 6 August 1945, the first time an atom bomb was ever dropped on a city. We call it the Thunderbolt. There was a mighty roar and our house collapsed. The blast threw me across the room, but, luckily, none of us were badly hurt. My mother and grandmother ran with me and my older brother to the river, past ruined houses bursting into flames. When we got there, the city was burning on both sides of the river. My grandmother suddenly turned back and was never seen again. A friend helped the rest of us into an abandoned boat and we sat in the middle of the river, watching flames tower over us from both banks. The river was crowded with boats and people trying to save themselves. And an oily black rain was falling.

Two-thirds of our city was destroyed by the bomb and the fires that it started, and nearly a hundred and fifty thousand people either died or were badly hurt.

They tell me that my country helped to start the terrible Second World War, and that it went on for years. By 1945, although Japan had been almost completely defeated, its leaders refused to surrender. The Allies warned that it must, or face the worst, but the generals ignored the warning. The Allies, led by the United States, decided they must act on their warnings. Hiroshima was a military centre, so they chose it to show Japan the power of the atom bomb, to force us to surrender.

The war has been over for ten years, but still people old and young die of radiation poisoning. There are many children like me in hospital here. I used to play with them when I was better. I lost one of my friends a short while ago, a little five-year-old girl. She wasn't even

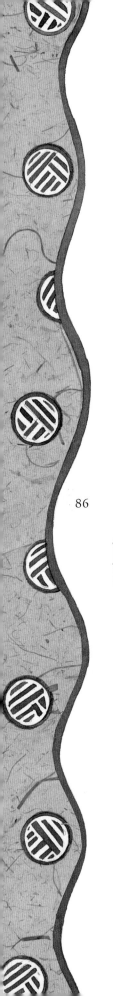

born when the bomb was dropped, but the poison in her mother's body passed into her. My friend Kiyo and I went to see her body, and she looked so peaceful, finally free from pain. Then we went up on the roof and looked at the stars. Maybe my friend is a star, now, too...

Although the war is over and the United States is helping Japan recover, the Thunderbolt still haunts our people. Our government has named 6 August Peace Day. On that day, we all go to the Peace Park. There are speeches and a memorial service. In the evening, there are fireworks. Afterwards families like ours go to the Ohta river near the

86

park to light little paper lanterns that we set on the water. We write the names of the family members who died in the blast, and the lanterns sail out to sea.

When I was well, I turned away from the scarred and limping people who had been badly injured by the Thunderbolt. I was more interested in the candyfloss and the fireworks. But now I am like those people.

When I began folding the cranes, all I wished for was to get well. Sometimes people do get better. But being here and seeing all the people who are sick like me has made my wish grow bigger. The night my friend died, looking up at the stars, I realised that I didn't want more people to die from A-bombs. You see, it's not enough to want myself to get better. I want the whole world to get over the sickness of the spirit that makes people hate and kill each other. I want peace for the whole earth. I wish I could write peace on the wings of every crane I fold and send them flying all over the world.

I am very weary now. Thank you for visiting me, and for this lovely paper. I'll make special cranes from it in honour of your visit, when I'm not so tired.

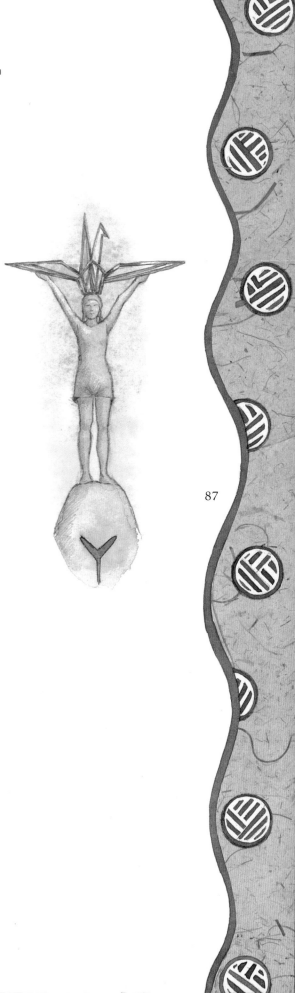

On 5 October 1955, Sadako went to sleep and never woke up again. She had completed 634 cranes. When they heard of her death, her classmates worked together as quickly as they could to make 356 more cranes so that their friend could be buried with a thousand cranes surrounding her. After her funeral, they collected all the letters she had written to them from the hospital and made them into a book that they sent all over Japan, to tell people about Sadako's special wish.

From that wish a dream grew, a dream that Sadako and the other children who died because of the atom bomb could have their own memorial in the Hiroshima Peace Park. Young people all over Japan collected enough money to build a statue of Sadako. It was unveiled in the Peace Park in 1958. The statue is of a girl standing on a granite base shaped like a mountain of paradise. Her hands are lifted up to hold a great golden crane. All over Japan children joined a growing Folded Crane Club, and every year on 6 August — Peace Day — they sent thousands of cranes to be placed at the foot of the statue, to spread Sadako's wish for world peace.

The story of Sadako spread all over the world, and children from other countries began to send paper cranes for Peace Day, too. Today, if you visit the Peace Park, you can see strings of paper cranes draped everywhere in Sadako's honour, but especially at the base of her statue. Engraved there is the wish that all these children share:

> *This is our cry, this is our prayer;*
> *peace in the world.*

87

AN ASIAN ACTIVIST

IQBAL MASIH
Pakistan

You are now paying your final visit — to a boy from the near past. It is early 1995, and you are in a town somewhere in Pakistan, a nation carved out of British-ruled India only fifty years ago. You are standing at the back of an old, run-down meeting hall, waiting to hear a speech given by the boy you are here to meet. His name is Iqbal Masih. As you look around at the crowd, you notice that most of the audience are young like you. But in all other ways, these children who stand there, quietly murmuring to each other, are not like you. Some have faces pinched with hunger, some bear scars on their bodies,

some are even bent over as if they are already very old. All of them are thin, poorly dressed, and their faces have lost the carefree innocence of youth. They look as though they have seen too much suffering, too young. They also look afraid.

Iqbal Masih enters with a few adults and is introduced by a man who praises his courage and intelligence. He reminds the audience that if anyone needs help, to please let him know, and he will do what he can. You cannot see Iqbal and have difficulty listening to his speech. It is hot in the room, people are shuffling about and there is no microphone. Even

so, you manage to catch most of what he is saying. He is telling these young people what their rights are. He says that if they are bonded workers, they are free now, they do not owe their masters any more labour, that it is not only wrong, it is against the law for their masters to mistreat and underpay them. He is telling them that they have the right to go to school, and that they can get help if they want it.

Some of the children leave before Iqbal has finished his speech. One whispers that she will be beaten if any-one finds out she has been here. Others stay to the end, and leave looking more hopeful than when they arrived. A few stay to talk to the adults who came with Iqbal, who have promised to help.

After everyone has left and quiet has fallen, Iqbal shakes hands with you and you stroll together through the town. He is a handsome boy, but his body has suffered. He is so small that he does not look twelve. His back is bent and there are scars on his arms and hands. Once outside, you walk slowly in the heat along a narrow lane with small, square-shaped houses on either side. Men ride by on bicycles, and a truck goes past, covered with elaborate, colourful decorations. Iqbal begins his story.

90

My story is just like the stories of the children you saw in the meeting hall. Only the details will differ. I come from a small country village in the Punjab, called Muridke. My eldest brother was getting married, and my parents had no money to pay for the wedding. So they accepted a loan from a man who said that they could pay it back by sending me to work in his carpet factory.

I was four years old when I went to work for him. I hardly ever saw my family after that. I was small and scared, and soon found out that I had reason to be. The factory owner knew that people like my parents have little or no education, so they cannot read a contract or bond, or even know there could be such a thing. So he had managed to trick my parents quite easily. The interest he was charging on the loan was more than he was 'paying' for my work. As a result, my parents' debt was increasing all the time.

The people who ran the factory were very cruel to me. At times they even chained me to a loom so I had to squat all day long to work. That is why my back is bent over, from not being allowed to stand up. And look at my hands: from tying many thousands of knots, they are all knotted, too. You'll notice that I wheeze a lot, from breathing in carpet dust day in day out for so many years.

There were other children besides me working in the factory as well. We had to work twelve to fourteen hours a day, seven days a week, with no time for going outdoors and playing, and we were beaten if our 'owner' thought we were

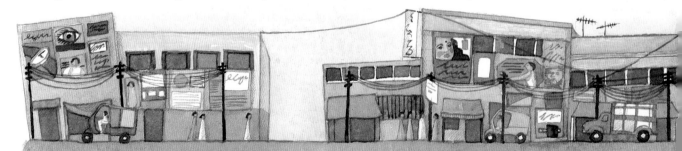

misbehaving. And of course we had no schooling whatsoever. They fed us very little and the food was poor quality without much nourishment in it. They even took the cost of the food out of our little pay, and we never got any money for ourselves because it was all going to pay the debts of our parents.

When I was ten, I was rescued from this life of pain and misery by a man called Ehsan Ulla Khan. In 1988 he founded the Bonded Labour Liberation Front (BLLF) to free children like me from bonded labour. I had gone to a meeting like the one you just saw, where I discovered that bonded child labour is illegal now. I was so moved on finding out about my rights that, before I knew it, I was standing up and making a speech at the meeting, a speech that was then printed in the newspapers! After that I refused to go back to my 'owner', and Ehsan Ulla Khan helped me get into one of the schools he had founded for children like me. I joined the BLLF, and by giving talks like the one tonight, I even helped other children escape from bonded labour.

I became one of the organisation's best speakers, and my speeches continued to be printed in the newspapers. I soon became famous, and I was sent to the United States and Europe to carry our message there. Just a little while ago, in December

1994, I received the Reebok Prize for Youth in Action. This is an international award! I am happy to be helping other children to gain their freedom and their rights. I think I have saved about 3,000 children so far.

Now that I am at school, I like studying and learning. One thing I am learning is more about child labour in my own country and in others. In Pakistan, although bonded child labour is now illegal, no one makes any arrests, and children are still working almost as slaves in many industries. The biggest employer of children is the carpet-weaving industry. Over a million children, and maybe many more, are doing this kind of work for pennies a day. Then the carpets are

sold in Europe and North America to rich customers who know no better. Not only does this go on in our country, but in India and Bangladesh as well.

And all over the world, children are doing other kinds of hard work for such long hours every day of the week. There are over 73 million children under the age of fourteen doing many different kinds of work. Most, but not all of them, live in Asia, Africa and South America. They are treated very badly, and then the things they make are sold in the rich Western countries.

These children are to be found in factories stuffing toys for big Western toy companies, or sewing sequins on fancy gowns or sharpening surgical instruments. Some of them work in dangerous places like glass or brick factories with no protection from sharp glass or hot furnaces, or they are put at risk making matches or fireworks. Some suffer horrible burns and yet they get no medical help. Many children also work from very young ages as servants for rich people, or they do farm work like cutting sugar cane, for many, many hours each day.

I have learned that child labour is growing all over the world in so-called

developing countries. It is true that poor families in poor countries need every member to help make a living. I think it is an honourable thing to work hard and take pride in work well done. And no matter whether they are rich or poor, all children who help their families can feel good about what they contribute.

But there is something very wrong when children are forced to work as hard or harder than grown-ups, and it is wrong for factory owners to steal us from our families with lies. Sometimes these factory people even kidnap children to work for them. When they begin to work, the youngest ones often receive no pay at all. I do not think that this helps poor families because it dooms their children to yet more poverty and ignorance.

Children are dying young from diseases caused by the work they are forced to do, or they are growing up crippled or shrunken like I am. They have no chance to go to school and be educated. If they were, they could do better kinds of work and they couldn't be cheated like my parents were. It cannot be right to beat us or brand us, or make us work while refusing to hire fully grown people. The main reason they want children, you see, is because we are small and helpless.

You can see that I get very angry when

I think of these things. But I know that my speaking out is making a difference. The carpet industry here is already losing millions of dollars because rich people in the West do not want to buy goods made by enslaved children. I am hoping that becoming famous will allow me to reach even more people around the world. To me, children are the future wealth of any country, and they should be free to grow up and be educated to do more than unskilled work.

I feel good about my own future. When I grow up, I want to become a lawyer, so I can help fight injustices against children. Right now my life is good, too. Now that I am free, I can see my mother and father again, and play with my cousins. I have a more normal life once more — if you don't count the death threats! The 'carpet mafia', we call them. They are angry factory owners who want to keep things the way they are and don't care at all about our welfare. I don't worry about these threats too much, though.

I see that I must go now. There are the other BLLF people waiting for me. I am glad to have met you. Go home and tell your families about what I have told you, OK? You can help too, you know. Goodbye!

93

Iqbal went home to visit his village of Muridke in the spring of 1995. On 16 April, he was riding a bicycle with two of his cousins when he was shot dead under mysterious circumstances. He was still only twelve years old.

His murder was never solved, but grave suspicion still rests on the 'carpet mafia'. Iqbal Masih had been so successful in exposing the evils of child labour that Pakistan lost about 14 million US dollars in sales in one year alone. If factory owners were behind the murder, it backfired, because sales dropped another 10 million dollars after the world heard the terrible news.

One person who learned about the murder of Iqbal Masih was another twelve-year-old boy — from Toronto, Ontario, in Canada. Craig Keilburger had never heard of Iqbal Masih before, but he was so upset when he read about the murder that he founded almost single-handedly a children's volunteer organisation to fight enforced child labour. It is called 'Free the Children'.

Craig's efforts to publicise the evils of child labour have been so successful that he has been able to travel around the world, speaking to heads of state and government agencies, and helping raise money for organisations like BLLF that free children and give them homes and education. One of the many ways he has helped 'free the children' has been to urge people to buy only carpets with a 'Rugmark' label. This guarantees that they are not made using child labour. Craig has founded branches of Free the Children in many countries.

There are many other organisations around the globe that work to end enforced child labour. Just a few of the other organisations are: UNICEF, through the United Nations; Child Rights Information Network in London, England; International Programme for the Elimination of Child Labour in Geneva, Switzerland; Set the Children Free in New Zealand; Community Aid Abroad in Australia; and US Child Labor Coalition in the USA. If you want to help out, too, you can contact one of them, or another organisation of your choice. One of the easiest ways to find these and similar organisations is to 'look on the Internet or to ask for help at your local library.

Iqbal Masih became a martyr for what he believed in, but he achieved something important both in life and in death. In life, he showed other children that just because they are small does not mean they are helpless.

He gave comfort and hope to other children like him, and helped them become free. Even his death could not stop the impact he made. His cause was taken up by others, including children in other, wealthy countries — children like Craig Keilburger. They too have discovered that they can do something to help the world, that they too can be young heroes.

SOURCES

* BOOKS FOR YOUNG PEOPLE. ! AUTHOR'S FAVOURITES.

ANNE FRANK

!Blair, Jon, *Anne Frank Remembered*, 1995. Academy Award-winning film documentary.
*!Frank, Anne, *The Diary of a Young Girl*, Doubleday, New York, 1967.
Frank, Anne, and the Netherlands State Institute for War Documentation, *The Diary of Anne Frank: The Critical Edition*, Doubleday, New York, 1986.
!Gies, Miep, *Anne Frank Remembered: The Story of the Woman who Helped to Hide the Frank Family*, Simon & Schuster, New York, 1987.
!!van der Rol, Ruud and Verhoeven, Rian for the Anne Frank House. *Anne Frank: Beyond the Diary, A Photographic Remembrance*. Viking, Penguin Group, 1993.

SUNDIATA

*!Chu, Daniel and Skinner, Elliott, *A Glorious Age in Africa*, Africa World Press, Trenton, 1992.
!Levitzion, Nehemiah, *Ancient Ghana and Mali*, Methuen & Co., London, 1973.
!Niane, D. T., *Sundiata: An Epic of Old Mali*, trans. G. D. Pickett, Longman, London, 1965.
*!Wisniewski, David, *Sundiata, Lion King of Mali*, Clarion Books, New York, 1992.

FANNY MENDELSSOHN

Elvers, Rudolf ed., *Felix Mendelssohn: A Life in Letters*, trans. Craig Tomlinson, Fromm International Publishing Corp., New York, 1986.
!Jacob, Heinrich Edouard, *Felix Mendelssohn and His Times*, Barrie & Rockliff, London, 1959.
!Kaufman, Schima, *Mendelssohn: A Second Elijah*, Tudor Publishing Co., New York, 1934.
!Kupferberg, Herbert, *The Mendelssohns: Three Generations of Genius*, W. H. Allen, London and New York, 1972 .
!Marek, George R., *Gentle Genius: The Story of Felix Mendelssohn*, Funk & Wagnalls, New York, 1972.
Radcliffe, Philip, *Mendelssohn*, J. M. Dent & Sons, London, and Farrar, Straus & Giroux, New York, 1967.
Tillard, Francoise, translated by Camille Naish, *Fanny Mendelssohn*, Amadeus Press, Portland Oregon, 1996.

KING LOUIS IX AND QUEEN BLANCHE

!Bray, Anna Eliza, *The Good St Louis and His Times*, Griffin and Farran, London, 1870.
*Hubbard, Margaret Ann, *Saint Louis and the Last Crusade*, Vision Books, Toronto, 1958.
!John of Joinville, *The Life of Saint Louis*, trans. Ren — Hague, Sheed & Ward, London, 1955. Written by a personal friend of King Louis.
Labarge, Margaret Wade, *Saint Louis*, Little, Brown & Co., Boston, 1968.

MILAREPA

Chang, Garma C. C. (trans.), *The Hundred Thousand Songs of Milarepa*, vols 1 and 2, University Books, Seacaucus, 1962.
!Lhalungpa, Lobsang P. (trans.), *The Life of Milarepa*, E. P. Dutton, New York, 1977.
Nalanda Translation Committee, directed by Chögyam Trungpa, *The Rain of Wisdom*, Shambhala Publications, Boston, 1980.

POCAHONTAS

*!Adams, Patricia, *Pocahontas, Indian Princess*, Dell Publishing Co., New York, 1987.
*Fritz, Jean, *The Double Life of Pocahontas*, G. P. Putnam's Sons, New York, 1983.
*Gleiter, Jan and Thompson, Kathleen, *Pocahontas*, Steck-Vaughn Co., Austin, 1991.
*!Iannone, Catherine, *Pocahontas: The True Story of the Powhatan Princess*, Chelsea House, New York, 1996.
*Jassem, Kate, *Pocahontas, Girl of Jamestown*, Troll Associates, Mahwah'N.J., 1979.
*!Raphael, Elain and Bolognese, Don, *Pocahontas, Princess of the River Tribes*, Scholastic, New York, 1993.

ANNE SULLIVAN AND HELEN KELLER

*!Davidson, Margaret, *Helen Keller's Teacher*, Scholastic, New York,1965.
*Graff, Stewart and Polly, *Helen Keller: Toward the Light*, Dell Publishing, New York, 1965.
*!Keller, Helen, *The Story of My Life*, Doubleday, Page, New York, 1903.
Lash, Joseph, *Helen and Teacher*, Delacorte Press, New York, 1980.
*!St George, Judith, *Dear Dr Bell...Your Friend, Helen Keller*, G. P. Putnam's Sons, New York, 1992.
*Waite, Helen Elmira, *Valiant Companions: Helen Keller and Anne Sullivan Macy*, Macrae Smith Co., Philadelphia, 1959.
*!Wepman, Dennis, *Helen Keller*, Chelsea House , New York, 1987.

DAVID

*de Regniers, Beatrice Schenk, *David and Goliath*, The Viking Press, New York, 1965.
*Fisher, Leonard Everett, *David and Goliath*, Holiday House, New York, 1993.
Heaton, E. W., *Everyday Life in Old Testament Times*, B. T. Batsford, London, 1956.
*Kent, David, *Kings of Israel*, Warwick Press, New York, 1982.
The New English Bible, 2 Samuel, Cambridge University Press, 1971.
Parmiter, Geoffrey de C., *King David*, Arthur Barker, London, 1960.

WILMA RUDOLPH

*Jacobs, Linda Altman, *Wilma Rudolph, Run for Glory*, EMC Corp., St Paul, 1975.
*!Krull, Kathleen, *Wilma Unlimited*, Harcourt Brace & Co., New York, 1996.
*Sherrow, Victoria, *Wilma Rudolph, Olympic Champion*, Chelsea House, New York, 1995.

ALEXANDER GRAHAM BELL

Bruce, Robert V., *Alexander Graham Bell and the Conquest of Solitude*, Little, Brown & Co., Boston, 1973.
*Langille, Jacqueline, *Alexander Graham Bell*, Four East Publications, Tantallon, 1989.
*!Quackenbush, Robert, *Ahoy! Ahoy! Are You There?*, Prentice-Hall, Englewood Cliffs, 1981.
Webb, Michael, *Alexander Graham Bell*, Copp Clark Pitman, Toronto, 1991.
*!Wing, Chris, *Bell at Baddeck*, Christopher King, Baddeck (private publication), 1980.

SADAKO SASAKI

*Coerr, Eleanor, *Mieko and the Fifth Treasure*, Dell Publishing Co., New York; *!*Sadako and the Thousand Paper Cranes*, Dell Publishing Co., New York, 1977. This was also made into a video of the same name, published by Informed Democracy, Santa Cruz, 1990.
!Hersey, John, *Hiroshima*, A. A. Knopf, New York, 1985.
Nasu, Masamoto, *Children of the Paper Crane*, M. E. Sharpe, Inc., Armonk, New York and London, 1991

IQBAL MASIH

Cummings, David, *Pakistan*, Wayland Publishers, Hove, UK,1989.
Lye, Keith, *Take a Trip to Pakistan*, Franklin Watts, London and New York, 1984.

———

US Department of Labor, Bureau of International Labor Affairs (ILAB) press releases: 'ILAB, International Labor Organization Sign Agreement to Develop Programs to Eliminate Child Labor', 7 August 1995; 'Labor Department Funds Grant on Eradication of Child Labor', 30 May 1996; 'Secretary Reich to Address World Labor Officials on Eradication of Child Labor', 10 June 1996.
Donovan, Paul, 'Carpet mafia: campaigner killed for speaking out', *New Internationalist*, October 1995, p. 4.
Articles by unnamed staff reporters:
'Battled child labour, boy, 12, murdered', *Toronto Star*, 19 April 1995, pp. A1, A24. 'Carpet trade hit by boy's murder', *Toronto Star*, 4 May 1995, p. A21. 'Indian children decry murder of young crusader', *Globe and Mail Metro Edition*, 20 April 1995. 'Kids at work: child labor is on the rise as countries rush into the global economy', (*Maclean's*' Toronto edition), 108/50, 11 December 1995, pp. 28—30. 'Wunderkinder: Craig Keilburger heads an international organization, influences Canadian government policy, testifies to US Congressional Committees...' *New Internationalist*, July 1997, pp. 28—9.

———

International Child Labor Study Office (www.dol.gov/dol/ilab/public/media/reports/sweat/main.html): *By the Sweat and Toil of Children: A Report to Congress by Bureau of International Labor Affairs*, US Department of Labor, 15 July 1994.
Pakistan Students Association (www.rpi.edu/dept/union/paksa/www.html/pakistan/carpet.html): Hand Knotted Carpet Industry Third World Traveler (www.infoasis.com/people/stevetet/Heroes/Iqbal—Masih.html): Carpets from Pakistan; Iqbal Masih — Pakistan; Killing for carpets — slavery and death in Pakistan's carpet industry,' Free the Children: an interview with Craig Keilburger', *Multinational Monitor*, January/February 1997.

walk
the way of wonder...
Barefoot Books

The barefoot child represents the person who is in harmony with the natural world and moves freely across boundaries of many kinds. Barefoot Books explores this image with a range of high-quality picture books for children of all ages. We work with artists, writers and storytellers from many traditions, focusing on themes that encourage independence of spirit, promote understanding and acceptance of different traditions, and foster a life-long love of learning.

www.barefoot-books.com